D1134202

A colour guide to familiar

MARSHLAND AND FRESHWATER BIRDS

A colour guide to familiar

MARSHLAND AND FRESHWATER

BIRDS

By Jiří Felix

Illustrated by Květoslav Hísek

Translated by Olga Kuthanová
Graphic design: Soňa Valoušková

English version first published 1975 by
OCTOPUS BOOKS LIMITED
59 Grosvenor Street, London W1

Reprinted 1977, 1978

© 1975 Artia, Prague

All Rights Reserved. No part of this publication may be reproduced or transmitted in any form or by any means, electronic or mechanical, including photocopy, recording, or any information storage and retrieval system, without permission in writing from the copyright owner.

ISBN 0 7064 0407 6

Printed in Czechoslovakia
3/10/09/51-03

CONTENTS

FOREWORD

Birds and their life both on land and in the air have always been of interest to people from all walks of life, but most of all to nature-lovers — both laymen and experts, and it is for these that this book is intended. Described here in words and pictures are sixty-four species of birds that inhabit inland waters, swamps and meadows near water. Some of these birds may, of course, be found also on the seacoast and vice versa, many sea birds wend their way inland, mostly during the winter months, and some even nest there. More about all these birds may be found in a separate chapter of this book.

Near water one may, of course, come across other species of birds classified under other habitats, for example the pied wagtail, fieldfare, kestrel, cuckoo, etc. Naturally certain birds occur in other places besides their typical habitat quite regularly and in large numbers during certain seasons: one such example is the common swallow, which in the autumn roosts in large flocks in reeds bordering ponds and lakes, etc.

The introductory section of this book acquaints the reader briefly with the structure and physical features of birds and their way of life. Separate chapters deal with those birds that in recent years have settled permanently in new localities, either farther south or north of their original homes, and birds that regularly visit inland waters during migration or for the winter. Also included are items about water game birds and the protection of waterfowl.

Illustrated in the pictorial section are the individual species, usually showing the male in breeding plumage. In those instances where the coloration of the male differs from that of the female both are generally shown. Each colour plate also includes an illustration of the typical egg of the given species and sometimes a drawing of the nest. The text accompanying each plate gives the basic biological data about the given species, items of interest about its way of life, a description of the nest, a verbal transcription of its voice and the dimensions of the egg. Also given is the average length of the bird in centimetres, measured from the tip of the bill to the tip of the tail, and sometimes also the wingspan or the flight contour.

INTERESTING FACTS
ABOUT THE PHYSICAL CHARACTERISTICS
OF WATERFOWL

Birds whose way of life is more or less permanently bound to water exhibit corresponding adaptations of body structure, limbs, bill, plumage, and the like.

The body of a bird is covered with feathers, which in most species grow in definite tracts called *pterylae*, the intervening spaces being termed *apteria*. The latter, however, are concealed by feathers and are thus not evident at first glance. The feathers that give the body its typical shape are called contour feathers, e. g. the flight feathers and tail feathers.

In ducks the flight feathers, when the bird is not airborne, are protected and kept from becoming waterlogged by a sort of feathered pocket into which the bird slips its wings. Underneath the contour feathers the body is usually covered with a layer of soft down feathers, which play an important role during the nesting period of certain water birds. The feathers of waterfowl are very thick and pressed close to the body. They must furthermore be well oiled so as not to become waterlogged. Serving this purpose is the uropygial gland located on the back, at the base of the tail feathers, which is particularly well developed in ducks and grebes. The oily fluid secreted by this gland is spread over the feathers by the bird with its bill, those covering the head are oiled by rubbing the head over the back feathers, the whole surface thus being perfectly impregnated. Water birds repeat this process several times a day. This, however, is not the only care required by the feathers. They must also be regularly wetted, together with the skin, to keep the former from drying out and the latter from cracking. For this reason water birds bathe thoroughly and then carefully preen their feathers several times a day. It is interesting to note that when wetting their feathers ducks and geese perform what might be termed group games, ruffling their feathers and slapping the water with their wings so that it penetrates more easily to the skin, and also diving below the surface. Such bathing games also occur with domesticated geese when they swim out onto a pond or stream. At first the flock swims about quite peacefully. Then suddenly one of the geese spreads its wings, flaps them against the water and dives just below the surface, even though geese are non-diving birds. This generally creates a chain reaction and the remaining geese also begin diving, flapping their wings, spraying water and ruffling their feathers. After a while the flock calms down and the birds flap their wings more slowly. When they have finished their bath they climb out of the water onto dry ground, where they shake and pinch their feathers with their bills to remove the water. Ducks also make jerking movements with their partly-spread wings to dry the feathers, after which they ruffle and oil the feathers and then trim and smooth them. This fact should be known to those who keep and breed various ducks and water birds in captivity, where they must always be supplied with clean water. Without it the ducks' feathers lose their oiliness and begin to stick together within a very few days. Such birds often make bathing movements on dry land and when they finally do swim out on water their feathers become soaked and so waterlogged that they lose the strength to climb out of the water and eventually drown.

Young water birds also need a regular bath at least once a day. However, their uropygial gland does not begin to function until their contour feathers begin to grow, although the down feathers of goslings, ducklings and young grebes also need to be oiled to prevent them becoming waterlogged. This problem is solved by the young climbing through the feathers of their parents, which are more intensively oiled at this time, thereby lubricating their own down. As the habit of preening is an innate one which they possess from birth, they spread their parents' oil evenly over their whole bodies. Without this lubrication the young would soon become soaked, then chilled, and finally would drown. That is why young goslings or ducklings raised in captivity without a mother should be given only shallow bowls of water into which flat stones have been put so that if soaked they may easily climb out. They cannot be allowed to swim in deep water by themselves until their uropygial gland is functioning perfectly.

Underneath the contour feathers of geese and ducks is a thick layer of down feathers, which serve as heat insulation.

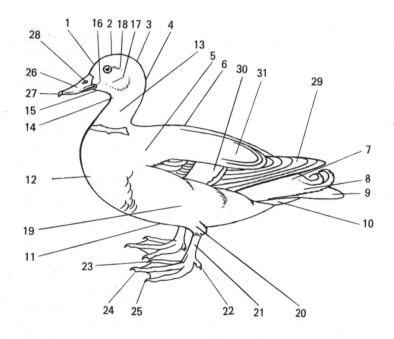

Fig. 1. Bird topography: 1) forehead, 2) crown, 3) hind neck, 4) nape, 5) shoulder, 6) back, 7) rump, 8) upper tail coverts, 9) tail feathers, 10) under tail coverts, 11) belly, 12) breast, 13) neck, 14) throat, 15) chin, 16) lores, 17) cheek, 18) ear region, 19) flank, 20) shank, 21) tarsus, 22) hind toe, 23) inner toe, 24) middle toe, 25) outer toe, 26) bill, 27) nail, 28) nostrils, 29) primaries, 30) secondaries, 31) shoulder coverts.

During the nesting period the hen plucks the down feathers from her belly to line the edges of the nest and to cover the eggs during her temporary absence, for they prevent rapid loss of heat from the incubated eggs.

A bird's feathers are replaced regularly by the process of moulting. Old feathers are shed and new ones grow in, pushing the old ones out. Whereas in most birds, such as songbirds, pigeons, gallinaceous birds, etc. the flight and tail feathers are shed successively so that the bird does not lose the power of flight, in many species of water birds, such as ducks, geese and crakes, the flight feathers are shed all at once so that the birds are incapable of flight for a certain period, usually three to seven weeks, during which they conceal themselves in reeds and rushes or other hiding places. Thus, for instance, drakes, which do not take care of the young, moult sooner than ducks, which shed their feathers after the young have reached maturity. On the other hand, both swan partners attend the young, and it is the female that moults first while the male protects the cygnets, after which it is his turn to moult. Their new flight feathers attain their full length at the same time as those of their offspring and then the whole family is able to set out on its migratory flight south.

In some species the coloration of the male's plumage differs markedly from that of the female. This is known as sexual dimorphism. In water birds this difference is especially marked in ducks and shelducks whereas male and female geese, swans and gulls have similar plumage.

Many species of birds have two differently coloured sets of plumage a year, which means that they moult twice yearly, the first being a complete and the second a partial moult. Ducks, for example, shed both the contour as well as flight feathers in spring. At this time the drake loses his bright nuptial plumage and resembles the female, but the newly emerging flight feathers are again brightly coloured, thus making it possible to distinguish between the two. Ducks moult a second time in the autumn, when they once more shed the small contour feathers but not the flight feathers.

At this time the male acquires a new bright nuptial garb, which he retains until the spring of the following year. In some individuals the moult takes longer, in others a shorter time and thus in the autumn one may often see amongst the brightly coloured drakes of a given species ones that have not yet completed their moult.

Many species of waders, for instance, have a different winter plumage, the difference being particularly striking in the case of the ruff. The nuptial dress of the male is very colourful and in addition he sports a broad, brightly coloured collar or ruff, hence his name. In summer, however, he sheds his bright plumage as well as the long feathers of the ruff and by autumn he acquires a new garb resembling that of the female. Also some species of grebes have brightly coloured nuptial plumage, worn by both male and female. The great crested grebe, for example, also has a broad ruff at this time.

The black-headed gull has a nuptial as well as non-breeding plumage; in winter its chocolate-coloured head turns white but in spring the white feathers are soon shed and replaced by the characteristic chocolate-brown ones. Also certain herons have a brightly coloured breeding plumage, e.g. the night heron and others.

The feet of water birds also vary according to the way of life of the species. The feet of the Anatidae family (swans, geese and ducks), have three front toes which are connected by a broad web and a fourth, hind toe located somewhat higher than the others. When swimming, the feet move alternately backward and forward as when walking; during the backward movement the webbed toes are spread far apart, whereas when the foot moves forward the toes are drawn together and the toe joints bend so that the surface area, and thus the resistance to the water, is as little as possible. When diving, e.g. in the case of diving ducks, the feet work differently. Because the duck is lighter than water it must overcome the upward hydrostatic pressure. Before submerging it exhales and presses its feathers tightly to its body to squeeze out air remaining in the plumage. Then it gives a sharp push with both legs, jumps above the surface and slips down under the water, keeping its feet above the body, i.e. above its centre of gravity. The farther the feet are stretched above the body the deeper the bird can dive, whereas when they are close to the body the bird moves forward in a horizontal direction. The driving power that propels the bird downward or forward is exerted by kicking the legs outward and backward somewhat as in the breast-stroke, with the webbed toes spread wide. As the feet move back under the body the toes are drawn together.

It is interesting to note that the ducklings of non-diving ducks are good at diving and do so when danger threatens. However, even the adults of certain non-diving birds will dive when in truly great danger, e.g. the ruddy shelduck, which dives and even swims several yards underwater in such a case. These birds, however, only swim just below the surface.

The grebes are completely adapted to a permanent life on water and dive well and to great depths. Even a day-old nestling dives adroitly. When swimming these birds float fairly low down in the water and when danger threatens can submerge their bodies even more. From this position they can disappear below the surface in a flash, and can stay under for up to a minute, swimming as much as fifty yards in that time. Unlike members of the Anatidae family the web of the grebe's foot is not complete; each of the three front toes is fringed separately.

Members of the rail tribe (family Rallidae), such as the coot, which spends most of its life on water, also have separately fringed toes. Other species of rail have fairly long legs with long toes adapted for running over stems or leaves of aquatic plants. Moreover, their bodies are very slim to enable them to move with ease through reeds and dense vegetation. All rails, of course, can also swim.

Waders are generally adapted to life at the water's edge, in shallows, swamps and mud flats. Some species, however, inhabit dry localities far from water. These small birds often have legs that are very long in proportion to the body. Most have webless toes, though some have a small web at the base of the toes, e.g. the avocet. The phalaropes have their toes fringed with a leathery web, as in coots. They, too, are mostly to be found on the surface of water, where they forage for food. Most species of waders generally keep to the shallow waters of the shore or the edges of water in swamps, etc.

Very long legs are a characteristic of the Ciconiiformes, which include the herons, storks, ibises and spoonbills. Some, such as the stork or grey heron, can easily stand and hunt prey in deeper water, though these birds also forage for food on dry ground.

Gulls, skuas and terns also have developed webs and move adroitly on the water surface; however, they do not float as low down in the water as ducks and their long wings indicate that they are first and foremost birds of the air.

Specially adapted toes are even to be found in one bird of prey that hunts over water, namely the osprey or fish hawk. It has a reversible outer toe and when catching fish grasps its prey with its opposable toes—two at the front and two at the back. Moreover, the toes have very long, curved claws.

The bills of many species of water and swampland birds are specially adapted to the kind of food they eat. Members of the Anatidae family have a characteristic nail, or horny plate, at the tip of the bill, the upper and lower edges of which are serrated. This horny plate begins to appear in the young at about the age of one week. The notches on the edges of the bills of geese are very hard and short, useful for nipping off plants, which form a large part of the goose's diet. The serrated edge of the duck's bill serves to sieve food; as the duck dabbles its bill in mud or water it moves its tongue in such a way as to create a vacuum and as the water flows in the small crustaceans, worms, etc. in it are sieved and trapped at the edges. With its sensitive tongue the duck then picks out the edible bits while the mud and water flow out again at the sides of the bill. There may be a great many such notches on the edges of the bill. The shoveler has as many as 180 on the upper bill alone. Mergansers have long, narrow bills with sharp, hooked notches

14

that enable the birds to get a better grasp on the small fish they eat.

Herons have a long, pointed bill which they often use as a spear when hunting. They also use it as a weapon of defence and are capable of inflicting quite serious wounds, usually aiming at the eyes. For that reason care must be taken when catching a heron by hand.

Storks, too, have a long, straight and pointed bill. The bill of ibises is down-curved like a sickle and used to gather food. The spoonbill's one is rather unusual; it is long and straight but wide and flattened at the tip. Spoonbills dabble in the mud or shallow water like ducks. Grebes have a fairly long bill with a sharply pointed tip, specially adapted for catching fish.

The bills of waders are for the most part fairly long, which enables them to forage for food in deep mud, water, wet marshy meadows, and the like. The oystercatchers' bills are strong, quite long, and slightly compressed at the sides to help them open the shells of bivalve molluscs or to plunge into sand or mud to bring up various worms, crustaceans and molluscs. Plovers, unlike other waders, have a fairly short bill. Members of the Scolopacidae family have very long bills, one of the most specialized being that of the snipe. Its tip is equipped with tactile cells, which make it possible for the bird to probe deep in the mud and capture its prey without seeing it. Snipes are able to open their bills and grasp food even in mud, but this ability is possessed by some other birds as well.

Curlews have a long bill curved like a sabre. The avocet's bill is long and thin with a slight upward curve which serves for hunting crustaceans in shallows, the bird's habit being to swing the bill from side to side to stir up the water for small crustaceans, which it then skilfully catches.

Gulls have beaks with sharp edges and a hooked tip, which is evidence of their predatory way of life. Terns, on the other hand, have straight, narrow, pointed bills which they use with great skill to catch fish.

MIGRATION

Waterfowl, like other birds, can be divided roughly into three groups according to whether they remain in their breeding grounds or depart for the winter. These are: resident birds that never leave their nesting grounds, staying even in winter; dispersive birds which after the nesting period spread far and wide throughout the countryside, often hundreds of miles from their breeding territory; migratory birds that leave their nesting grounds each year, usually in the autumn, flying to areas farther south (birds of the southern hemisphere fly north) and returning again in the spring.

Within one and the same species, however, there may be various populations, some of which are resident, others transient migrants and still others migratory birds. One such water bird is the mallard. In some parts of Europe members of a given species may be resident, this usually being so in the case of populations nesting in western or southwestern Europe, whereas members of the same species inhabiting northern Europe are migrant. Then again, in some species, for example certain species of duck, populations from the north move southward for the winter, say to central Europe, whereas central European populations move to southern Europe. Sometimes, however, even birds that are otherwise resident in specific areas will suddenly set out in large flocks in a southerly or southwesterly direction. These are called irruptive migrants and include among their number the nutcracker and long-eared owl.

Birds of Europe migrate in three main directions: southwest, south and southeast, depending on where the individual species or their populations nest. The route of the autumn flight and return flight in spring need not always be the same. Some birds winging their way to their winter quarters may choose a lengthier route along the seacoast whereas in spring

Fig. 2. Migrating swans.

they return by a shorter, more direct route, e.g. north via central Europe.

The migration of many species of birds encompasses a broad front, though in some places it narrows, for instance in the case of some barrier such as a range of high mountains, when the birds seek more convenient routes, e.g. mountain passes, river valleys and the like, and converge in greater numbers. Birds also fly en masse across sea straits, where they often form huge flocks. Birds whose way of life confines them to water generally keep to rivers, lakes or streams, sometimes also migrating along the seacoast.

Many Europan birds winter no farther than western and southwestern Europe or the Mediterranean region, e.g. the tufted duck. Other water birds that winter in western and southwestern Europe are the grey lag goose, pintail and wigeon. The Mediterranean and North Africa are the winter quarters of the gadwall, teal, garganey and shoveller. Some

Fig. 3. Migrating cranes.

of these species of ducks from more northerly regions, how-ever, have recently begun also to winter in central Europe, e.g. the tufted duck and teal. As can be seen, most European birds of the Anatidae family migrate southwest. The grey lag goose's populations nesting in Iceland fly straight south, of course, and winter in England.

Many other birds also take a southwesterly route, e.g. the grey heron, which winters in southwestern and central Europe but also as far away as North Africa. The night heron and little bittern, however, fly all the way to equatorial Africa.

Eastern and southern Africa are where the white stork spends the winter, flying there from Europe via two main routes — southeast and southwest, and only sometimes di-rectly south. Western populations journey across Spain and Morocco. Eastern stork populations journey southeast across the Bosphorus and Asia Minor to Africa, proceeding onward chiefly along the Nile. This is the path of the main stork mi-gration. On the territory between the Elbe and Rhine the populations intermingle and travel south along both main routes to eastern and southern Africa, which are the white stork's favourite winter haunts. During the autumn migration the storks fly about 60 to 75 miles a day and during the return trip in spring the average is over 90 miles per day.

The migratory flight of most birds is not very fast; usually they fly only a few hours a day, though some seabirds, such as terns and waders, are known to fly far greater distances in that time. The return trip from the winter quarters to the breeding territory is usually about a third faster for the birds are in a hurry to get to their nesting grounds. However, even during this period the flight may be influenced and slowed down by the sudden onset of bad weather, e.g. snowstorms and the like. Generally, though, variations in the time of arrival of most species of birds are very slight.

Some species migrate in flocks, e.g. geese, cormorants, ducks, cranes, waders, etc., some flying in their own typical formations, for instance cranes and geese. Other species make the flight alone, e.g. the cuckoo and golden oriole.

Migration is an inherited trait and even those birds that make the flight alone, including young ones making their first flight without the company of older and experienced birds, e.g. cuckoos or red-backed shrikes, find their way to their proper destination. In other species that fly in groups the young have an easier time, for they are guided by older birds that have made the trip there and back at least once before.

When migrating, birds generally use their sight for purposes of orientation, navigating chiefly by the sun, and at night by the moon and stars. There are, of course, other theories which assume that the orientation of at least some birds is determined by the earth's gravitational pull or by the magnetic pole. At the nesting site and in the surrounding neighbourhood birds find their way mainly by their memory of various landmarks.

LIFE IN THE NEST

On their arrival at the nesting grounds the birds select their mates, though in some species this may already have taken place in their winter quarters or on the return journey. The pairing is preceded by courtship, which may include various calls, spectacular flights, sometimes bordering on the acrobatic, rapid movements of the wings, nodding of the head, diving, etc. In the courtship display of the white stork, for instance, both partners clatter their bills loudly while laying their heads on their backs. The courtship antics of the great crested grebe are also interesting; the two partners swim towards each other, stretch their necks upwards and shake their heads briskly, then raise themselves erect above the water with chests pressed together, sometimes holding bits of water plants in their beaks. The courtship performance of cranes is also spectacular. They hop about and leap into the air, flap their wings and run rapidly around in circles, while making trumpet-like sounds. Their courtship is a veritable dance. As for cormorants, the male sits on the nest, raises his beak and tail straight up in the air, jerks his wings, and at the approach of a female abruptly lays his head on his back and emits a hollow sound. The female then comes towards him with the throat sac puffed up, raises the feathers on her head and utters sounds resembling grunts. The male heron holds himself erect, ruffles his feathers and snaps at the empty air with his beak. Courting swans swim towards each other and when close immerse their necks in the water, either separately or often intertwined. The courtship display of ducks as a rule is also very striking. In some species the male and female swim around each other, dive, shake their heads rapidly, frequently submerge their bills, abruptly raise themselves erect, lift their wings, stretch their necks out over the water, etc. There are many stages to the courtship performance of ducks. In species such as the goldeneye the males at one point throw their heads back sharply and jerk them rapidly a number of times, often spraying water behind them with their feet. A familiar sight is the courtship display of the ruddy shelduck; the drakes, whose nuptial plumage includes a broad ruff of feathers, wage symbolic duels during which they spread these coloured ruffs wide. The male snipe flies high in the air during courtship and then swoops down with tail feathers outspread; the loud drumming sound which can be heard far away as he plummets downwards is caused by the vibration of the outermost tail feathers. Gulls, too, have their characteristic courtship performance, during which the partners stand facing each other, raise their heads upwards, open their bills wide and utter loud calls, droop their wings, spread their tail feathers, bow to each other, shift their weight from one foot to the other, etc.

Each species has its characteristic manner of courtship. In some, as has already been said, it is very striking and attracts notice from afar whereas in others it is fairly inconspicuous.

Prior to nesting, birds stake out a specific area, called the nesting ground or territory, which they defend against all intruders, especially ones of their own kind. Songbirds proclaim ownership of their territory by their characteristic song, owls by hooting, male cuckoos with their cuckoo song, etc. Some species of birds nest in colonies and their nesting territory is limited only to the actual nest and its immediate vicinity. Birds living on or near water include many species that are colonial nesters, often forming very large colonies. Some of these colonies may be mixed, that is, they may consist of several species of birds. Thus, for instance, grey herons and night herons form not only independent but also mixed colonies, being often joined by spoonbills, cormorants, and other species. Dense colonies are frequently formed by gulls, their nests packed tightly together, though at other times they may be spaced several yards apart, depending on the nesting opportunities and number of pairs in the colony.

Some birds are fond of forming their own smaller colony within a colony of gulls or close beside it, for example certain species of terns, which feel safer close by their stronger and more alert kin. Large colonies are formed by the black-necked grebe, and the great crested grebe also forms colonies at times, generally, however, on bigger lakes where the larger hunting ground provides ample food for all. Such colonies are not to be found on small ponds. Also, certain species of waders seek company during the nesting period and the nests of individual pairs are built only short distances from each other. Such behaviour, however, depends first and foremost on the nesting opportunities. Thus, for instance, the little winged plover usually nests separately in pairs. However, if the water of lakes or ponds rises and floods the banks, several pairs may then build their nests together in a spot suitable for this purpose. Ducks, too, often build their nests close to each other, thus forming a sort of colony, e.g. on a small island. One duck which does this is the tufted duck.

Prior to actual nesting the birds form pairs. Some species pair only during the courtship, after which each individual goes its own way, e.g. the cuckoo. In other species the partners remain together, some only for the duration of the nesting period, e.g. wrens, others for life, e.g. the grey lag goose and mute swan. In such species if one of the partners dies the other often remains alone. This is true mostly of older birds, but young ones usually find themselves a new mate. Some species of birds do not pair until they have attained full maturity, e.g. geese and swans not until the fourth or fifth year.

After the birds have paired, or after their arrival at the breeding grounds, the partners begin to build a nest, that is all except social parasites, such as cuckoos, which lay their eggs in the nests of other birds. Some ducks do this too, not always but sometimes, even though they are not true social parasites.

Building a nest is an inherited trait and birds do not need to be taught how. Each species builds a particular type of nest which can generally be easily identified as belonging to that particular species. Some, mostly songbirds, e.g. warblers, build very complex structures that are almost works of art. Others, such as the night heron, build simple nests of only a few sticks. Woodpeckers hollow out cavities, whereas other birds seek out a ready-made cavity. Such species of water birds which do this, for instance, are the goldeneyes and mergansers. The nest is generally built by the female, and only on rare occasions by the male alone. In some species both partners share the task of construction, which in the case of small birds takes about a week and in the case of larger birds up to several weeks. Many birds build a new nest before every breeding season, others use the same nest for a number of years, adapting or adding to it every year, e.g. the white stork, white-tailed eagle, and others. Birds dependent on water in one way or another naturally build their nests on or near it. Some, for instance grebes, build their nests directly on the water, usually concealed in reeds, rushes etc. Grebes' nests are often waterlogged and the eggs are constantly damp. However, most birds, even waterfowl, build their nests so that the eggs remain dry. All ducks build their nests on a dry foundation even though it may be situated above water, e.g. in bent and broken reeds and the like. On the other hand, ducks' nests may also be located quite a distance from water and some species even lay their eggs in tree hollows or the nests of predators, sometimes more than sixty feet above the ground. The newly hatched ducklings therefore fall from the nest to the ground. As a rule they are not harmed by such a fall because they are cushioned by their thick soft layer of down. Swans build their nests on bent reeds and also on islets, as does the grey lag goose, which on rare occasions may also build its nest in a tree, e.g. in a pollarded willow, usually in locations where regular spring floods might damage nests on water or on the ground. Herons and their allies build their nests in trees. Some species, however, nest in reed beds on old, bent reeds, this being a favourite location for the spoonbill's nest. Gulls build floating structures of bits of reeds, etc. directly on water, also on bent reeds, small islets, and even rocks.

Waders build their nests, often only sparsely lined, on the ground. They are often located close to water and are therefore frequently flooded as a result. If there are no eggs in the nest at that time waders, e.g. sandpipers, will build onto it if the water starts rising, erecting a chimney-like structure to keep the water out of the hollow where the eggs are laid.

The coloration and often the number of eggs are characteristic for each given species. Ducks, geese, herons and other birds have plain eggs — white, yellowish, pale brown, greenish, etc. In other species, however, the coloration of the eggs shows marked variation, e.g. those of gulls, spoonbills, etc. The eggs of birds nesting in cavities or of those that cover their eggs on leaving the nest are usually plain, often white. On the other hand, those of birds that nest in open places and do not cover their eggs have protective coloration, e.g. gulls, spoonbills and waders.

The full clutch of some species always contains a set number of eggs. For instance, waders almost always lay four eggs, pigeons two, gulls three, etc. Ducks lay a greater number of eggs, usually about ten. However, as has already been said, the females of some species of duck behave as social parasites and lay their eggs in the nests of other ducks. The red-crested pochard is a common example, though other ducks are known to do it, too. Most ducks, however, build their own nests and incubate the eggs themselves.

The eggs are incubated by the female alone (ducks and geese), or else the duties of incubation are shared by both partners (storks and herons). Only in rare instances is this task performed solely by the male — of European birds the dotterel and red-necked phalarope. The period or duration of incubation is usually between eleven and fourteen days in the case of smaller species and about twenty days in the case of larger species, e.g. about twenty-six days in ducks and twenty-eight days in geese. The newly hatched nestlings are generally cared for by both parents; in some species, however, only by the female and in exceptional cases only by the male.

Birds are divided into two basic groups according to the degree of their development at birth. The young of the first group are independent at birth and follow their parents about within a few hours after hatching. They feed themselves immediately and the parents merely provide them with protection against enemies, cold, rain, etc. In the case of ducks and grebes they also oil their offspring's feathers and guide them to food. The species whose young feed themselves from the moment of birth are called nidifugous birds.

A special group includes those birds that might be termed semi-nidifugous. Their young are capable of independent activity and run about, make their way through reeds and swim within a few hours of hatching. For the first few days, however, the parents bring them food, which the young take from their beaks. Rails are one such example. In some species of rails the fledglings of the first brood bring food to the offspring of the second brood. The young of these species, however, soon begin to forage for food themselves — when only a few days old.

Birds of the second group, higher on the evolutionary scale than the first, are called nidicolous species and their young are generally blind and without feathers on hatching, so that they are fully dependent on the care of the parents, who provide them with warmth, protection and food. Examples of such birds are herons, storks, kingfishers, songbirds and many others. However, there are also other species whose young are covered with a thick layer of down when they hatch, for example owls and raptors.

Then there is the group of birds that are true social parasites. These do not devote any care to their eggs whatsoever, depositing them in the nests of other birds, which then incubate them and attend upon the young. A typical social parasite amongst European birds is the cuckoo.

The young of nidicolous species demand food in various ways that urge the parents to greater activity. The most common method is by uttering loud cries. Another is visual; the young of many species have bright yellow gapes, coloured spots on the bills or luminous warty protuberances and the sight of these triggers off the required response in the adult birds. The third method is tactile — the young grasping at the beaks of the parents bringing them food, e.g. in herons. The adult birds of some species place the food directly into the beaks of their offspring; in other species, e.g. herons, the baby birds take the food from their parents' beaks themselves, and still other species regurgitate partially digested food from the crop into the nestlings' beaks or else into the nest where the young pick it up.

The parents also keep the nest clean. Many species, e.g. songbirds, remove the nestlings' droppings with their beaks and either throw them out or swallow them. The young of other birds drop their faeces over the edge of the nest or squirt it out, e.g. raptors. Only in some species do the droppings remain in the nest, the young birds sitting on top of the pile as it grows.

The time spent in the nest varies greatly. In the case of smaller songbirds it is usually twelve to twenty days, in larger songbirds about a month. The young of larger raptors, such as the osprey, remain about two months in the nest. Chicks of birds nesting in hollows remain there rather longer, e.g. the kingfisher and bee-eater nearly a month. The young of some large birds of prey, e.g. vultures, remain in the nest about 100 days and those of certain species of shearwaters and petrels as long as 240 days.

In many instances of birds that nest in colonies the nests are often crowded close together and there may be a great many of them on a fairly small area. Such colonies, e.g. those of gulls, may have as many as a thousand nests. How, then, do the birds recognize their own nest amongst such a vast number? Countless experiments have shown that gulls and other birds find their nests by their location, which they have fixed in their memory. It was also discovered that often the colour or shape of the eggs is of no importance. Gulls still settled on their nests even when they contained pebbles or other smooth, hard-edged objects put there in place of the eggs. Many birds build their nests near conspicuous objects, e.g. plovers close by a large stone, other birds beside a clump of timothy-grass, at the foot of a tree, beside a pole, etc., thereby being able to find them without any difficulty. Most birds, however, are not capable of distinguishing their own eggs in the nest.

How, then, do birds recognize their offspring? For instance young gulls that scatter when danger threatens and stray into other gulls' territory are not only chased by the other gulls but also pecked on the head and even killed by them. The same happens in other species of colonial nesters. It was discovered, however, that for five days following the hatching of their own offspring gulls will also feed the young of other species that have either strayed there or been put in the nest, but after that time they chase them out. Why they do this is very simple. The adult birds recognize the particular voice of their own progeny even amongst the many similar nestlings in the area. Hearing plays an important role in a bird's life. The parents are able to distinguish almost perfectly the voices of their young, which can be heard while they are still inside the egg. Parents also react immediately to the voice of a strayed nestling, even though they do not see it, whereas when a hen, used in experiments for this purpose, saw that its chick was in danger but could not hear it (the chick was placed under glass which muffled its voice) she made no response whatsoever.

How the young recognize their parents is another question. Most nestlings do not learn to recognize their parents until some little time after they have hatched. Ducklings, for example, learn to recognize their mother after eight to twenty hours. During this period the young birds impress the image of their parents on their memory and thereafter recognize them without fail. In captivity, however, the young often hatch in incubators and consequently consider as their parent, say, the person whose image they impress upon their memory during the first few hours of their life. Such behaviour is particularly striking in various species of geese, which view their keeper as a parent, respond to his voice and run to him when danger threatens. If a lone gosling has been reared by man without any of its siblings then when it reaches maturity it often views man, and not its own kind, as a partner for itself. Another example is the white stork. When reared by man from birth, it remains very tame throughout its whole life, approaching man as a partner and also greeting him with the characteristic clatter of the bill while laying its head on its back. In some species of birds the behaviour is even more complex, for instance in waders that have been artificially incubated and reared by man. At first they view human beings as parents but as they grow older estrangement follows. However, the birds remain quite tame. Other species of waders that have the innate habit of concealing themselves, e.g. the snipe, are much shyer. In the case of birds such as crows, jackdaws, etc., there may occur a switch in the object of their parent figure. Young jackdaws removed from the nest several days after hatching, when they have already come to know their parents well, soon replace these in their memory by the figure of the one who supplies them with food—i. e. man.

In some species of birds, for instance ducks, young drakes impress the likeness of the duck upon their memory not only as a mother but also as a female so that in the wild when the time comes, apart from the rare exception, they select a mate of their own kind. In captivity, on the other hand, especially in zoos, where many ducks are reared without parents, cross-breeding is quite common, even amongst non-related species. Sometimes an individual bird will even reject a partner of its own species with which it has been placed in a separate aviary but will mate with any species that has been in its company from the time of its birth.

Some birds that have been reared by man and have then found their own kind often continue to regard him as a member of their species and behave accordingly. For example, during the nesting period in captivity the males of various species of geese chase and attack not only other geese but also any human being that comes near the nest, whereas in the wild both the sitting goose and the gander standing guard would fly away in such a case.

FOOD

Marshland and water birds often acquire their food in unusual and characteristic ways. Some species feed on fish, others are omnivorous, still others feed on insects or plants. Then there are also food parasites, namely birds that obtain their food from other birds. Skuas are such an example. They harass gulls until they regurgitate their catch, which the skuas skilfully retrieve in the air and then eat. Naturally they forage for food on their own as well. Many species of waterfowl are fish-eaters or fish comprise at least part of their diet. Some birds dive quite deeply for fish, e.g. grebes and cormorants. Cormorants can remain underwater for as long as seventy seconds, grasping their prey from the side with the hook on their upper bill. Pelicans are specially equipped for hunting fish. They do not dive but dip their bills, which are fitted with a broad distensible pouch beneath the lower beak, into the water stirring up the fish, which they catch in their pouch rather like in a dip-net. As a rule, a flock of pelicans forms a semi-circle, which then swims as one chasing the fish towards the shallows where they are more easily caught, a method very similar to that used by fishermen catching fish in a net. The pelican is capable of catching and swallowing fish weighing up to four pounds. Herons, too, feed largely on fish, standing in a single spot in the shallows or else wading slowly through the water while keeping a sharp lookout. As soon as a fish comes close the heron makes a swift thrust with its pointed beak and spears its prey. The same method is also used to catch other small vertebrates. Storks are partial to frogs, small fish and other small vertebrates and various insects, which they hunt in the shallows or near water. They, too, forage for food walking at a slow pace or else standing still in a single spot. The spoonbill has a specially adapted beak, which is long and flattened and dilated at the tip into a spoon. It catches its prey (various water insects, crustaceans, etc., as well as the occasional small fish or amphibian) by wading along with its bill half immersed in the mud, swinging its head from side to side. Some birds of the Anatidae family, mainly ducks, use their bills to sieve plankton from the water. Some species of duck obtain their food by diving, others gather it on or just below the surface. Ducks feed on animal as well as plant matter. The diet of divers includes more animal food than that of surface-feeding ducks. Mergansers feed on marine plankton and small fish. Geese are mostly vegetarian and so are swans, but both will eat an animal on occasion, e.g. small molluscs and the like.

Some fish-eating birds capture their prey by plummeting into the water from the air. One such example is the king-fisher, which frequently dives with such force that it disappears under the water. Grasping the prey in its beak, it then flies up onto a branch to swallow it. The kingfisher often hovers motionless in a single spot above the water. Similar behaviour can be seen in the common tern, which also plunges into the water after its prey. A real fishing specialist is the raptorial osprey or fish hawk. This bird hovers above the water in a single spot until sighting its prey, then it plunges down after it and often disappears from view in the water. Unlike the other birds mentioned here, the osprey catches its prey with its long claws, sinking them into the victim's flesh and carrying it to a tree where it then eats it. It catches fish weighing as much as four pounds. The black kite, on the other hand, skilfully gathers dead fish floating on the water's surface, as well as other vertebrates and their remnants.

Rails gather food on the water's surface, in reeds, etc., their diet consisting mainly of insects, molluscs and spiders, as well as small seeds and bits of green plants. Waders forage for food in shallows or swamps, and sometimes also in fields and meadows near water. The little ringed plover, for instance, and some other species of waders, runs rapidly along the muddy shore or in the mud of the shallows, popping into its mouth any worm or insect larva that emerges from its hiding place in the mud.

Many birds capture their prey, mostly insects, on the wing above the water's surface. Examples are the house martin, sand martin, red-footed falcon and others. Water birds feeding primarily on insects include various species of warblers. The seeds of aquatic and marsh plants are the chief food of the reed bunting.

NEW SETTLERS

The composition of bird species in a given region may change over the years. Some may vanish from the area, others, totally new to the territory, may establish themselves there, and still others that were absent for a time may reappear again in their old territories if there are adequate nesting opportunities.

Man is responsible for the disappearance of many species of birds, some of which have become extinct, for example the great auk of northern Europe. Other species have disappeared because the large swamps and marshes which were their nesting grounds have dried up, for example the crane, abundant in England until the eighteenth century. Other species whose way of life was dependent on swampy locations have moved away from many parts of Europe for the same reason.

On the other hand, birds that never nested there previously are extending their range and becoming established in new territories. Some have even launched large-scale invasions. One such example is the collared turtle dove, originally a native of India, western and southern China. In the sixteenth century it was introduced into Asia Minor, where it soon spread to various cities. At the beginning of the twentieth century it began extending its range westwards and nowadays is one of the commonest birds in Europe, where, moreover, it remains throughout the winter.

Certain species of birds, however, were intentionally introduced by man to new environments, where they soon became acclimatized and since that time rank as members of the local avifauna. One such example is the pheasant, introduced as early as medieval times to central and western Europe, where it acclimatized itself to the new conditions and is now one of the commonest birds on the Continent.

One reason for the pheasant's excellent acclimatization, of course, is the fact that it is a poor flier and thus belongs to the resident species.

Nevertheless, during the past few decades many marshland and water birds that are migrants and known to be excellent fliers have settled in entirely new territories and established large populations there.

One species that has extended its range without man's intervention is the tufted duck *(Aythya fuligula)*, originally indigenous to northeastern Europe. In the late nineteenth century it began to spread to central Europe and today is one of the most frequent ducks seen on the ponds and rivers of that part of the Continent, especially in Germany, Poland and Czechoslovakia. However, it has not as yet become established in Austria or Hungary, but has been observed nesting irregularly in Switzerland, France, Yugoslavia, Bulgaria, Romania and also in Cyprus.

Another bird that is spreading its range, in this case northward, is the red-crested pochard *(Netta rufina)*, otherwise native to the islands of the Mediterranean, southeastern Spain and the northern parts of the Black and Caspian Seas. It now nests regularly in France, in the Rhône Valley, and has also appeared in several places in central Europe, where it occurs to date in smaller populations. It nests locally in Germany and Czechoslovakia and has also established nesting grounds in Denmark, Belgium and Holland.

One of the latest new settlers in central Europe is the goldeneye *(Bucephala clangula)*, a typical duck of northern Europe. It had already become established previously in some parts of northern Poland and the northern part of East Germany but in 1960 it extended its range as far as southern Bohemia, where its numbers have since shown a steady increase. It furthermore nests regularly in Great Britain and also in Switzerland.

Of the water birds that have become established in Europe through man's efforts the Canada goose *(Branta canadensis)* heads the list. This large goose, a native of North America, was raised in England as a semi-domesticated species from about the seventeenth century. Later it spread into the wild, where it now numbers more than three thousand birds, according to the experts' estimate. The English populations are resident and do not leave the country even during the winter months. The Canada goose was also introduced into Sweden, where it has likewise formed populations. These, however, are migrant and fly for the winter to Holland and Germany. In recent years the Canada goose has also appeared in other parts of central Europe.

During the past few years another increasingly frequent nester in certain parts of Europe has been the ruddy shelduck *(Tadorna ferruginea)*, which is indigenous to the western Mediterranean, Asia Minor and the desert lakes around the Aral Sea. Birds found nesting here and there in central and western Europe, however, are individuals that escaped from zoos or else were released voluntarily from captivity. We cannot speak of populations as yet, though these may become established some time in the future. Another increasingly frequent nester in central Europe is the mute swan *(Cygnus olor)*. Originally kept as semi-domesticated birds on the pools or small lakes of chateaux, large houses and parks, many young swans settled on lakes and ponds in the wild and began to nest there regularly. In some places, such as in the northern lake country of East Germany and Poland, however, the mute swan populations are indigenous.

Also certain birds of the heron tribe are beginning to extend their range to new places, though not to such an extent as birds of the Anatidae family. The purple heron *(Ardea purpurea)*, for instance, nests commonly in southern, southeastern and southwestern Europe and in the past few decades has been occurring with increasing frequency in central Europe, where, though still rare, it is already beginning to form regular populations. It nests, for instance, in Austria, Czechoslovakia, Switzerland and Holland. In the nineteenth century it also nested in certain parts of Germany but these nesting grounds have again been abandoned.

The night heron *(Nycticorax nycticorax)* is another bird that is becoming established in new areas in Europe with increasing frequency, as are also certain species of waders. One such example is the black-tailed godwit *(Limosa limosa)*, originally an inhabitant of northern Europe and nowadays fairly plentiful in many parts of central Europe. Other waders, for instance the Eurasian avocet *(Recurvirostra avosetta)*, nest occasionally on certain lakes in central Europe—they do not occur regularly nor do they form populations there.

WINTER VISITORS TO INLAND LAKES AND WATER COURSES

During the winter months the lakes of western and central Europe that do not freeze over are visited by waterfowl from Scandinavia, which winter there. Some species do so regularly and in large numbers whereas others are vagrants that appear singly and only on occasion, mostly those that winter on the seacoast and stray inland more or less by chance. Still others visit these localities for only a brief period, generally in autumn and early spring, on their migratory flights to southern Europe or Africa.

Winter visitors, then, are primarily birds that do not nest in the given territory but occur there outside the breeding season, mainly during the winter months. One example is the whooper swan *(Cygnus cygnus)*, which nests in northeastern Europe and winters regularly on the coasts of Scandinavia, Great Britain, the Baltic Sea, North Sea, Black Sea and Caspian Sea. However, when there are hard frosts in their regular winter quarters small flocks of these swans also appear inland in central Europe on rivers that do not freeze over.

The northernmost parts of Asia and Greenland are the home of the brent goose *(Branta bernicla)*, which leaves its breeding grounds to winter in the British Isles and on the coasts of western and northwestern Europe. Frequently, however, it strays inland into central Europe, but only in small flocks. Another, but very rare, visitor to central Europe is the barnacle goose *(Branta leucopsis)*, which likewise winters regularly in the British Isles and northwestern parts of West Germany. It, too, is a bird of the far north, nesting in Norway, Greenland and Spitsbergen.

The British Isles, southern, southwestern and western Europe are the winter quarters of the white-fronted goose *(Anser albifrons)*, which nests on the coast of Greenland and in the northernmost parts of northeastern Europe. Flocks of these geese may also be seen frequently on inland ponds, especially in the autumn, when they pass through on their migratory flight south. Central, western and southern Europe serves as the winter quarters of the bean goose *(Anser fabalis)*, which nests in the far northern parts of Europe and Asia. The other species of Scandinavian geese visit central Europe only sporadically.

Of the Scandinavian ducks the scaup *(Aythya marila)* winters in large numbers in the British Isles, the Mediterranean region and on the coast of western Europe, the North Sea and the Baltic Sea. During the period of its migration to these winter quarters it can also be seen on the ponds and rivers of central Europe.

The goldeneye *(Bucephala clangula)* is also a regular winter guest in western, central and southern Europe. At this time small groups of these ducks, mostly from northern Scandinavia, may be seen on large rivers.

Other Scandinavian ducks that spend the winter on the coast of western Europe are the long-tailed duck *(Clangula hyemalis)*, the velvet scoter *(Melanitta fusca)* and the black scoter *(Melanitta nigra)*. These ducks occur rarely but at regular intervals in central Europe on rivers that do not freeze over during the winter months.

A solitary, but comparatively frequent, winter visitor to the interior is another duck of the north—the eider *(Somateria mollissima)*, though its regular winter quarters are located in the North Sea and Baltic Sea area.

Frequent and regular winter visitors to the inland rivers of central, western and southern as well as southeastern Europe are the mergansers of Scandinavia. The ones most often seen there are the red-breasted merganser *(Mergus serrator)* and the goosander *(Mergus merganser)*, though the smallest of them all, the smew *(Mergus albellus)*, which breeds in the northernmost parts of northern Europe, also appears there regularly.

Further regular winter visitors to the rivers of central and western Europe include two species of Scandinavian divers, namely the black-throated diver or loon *(Gavia arctica)* and the red-throated diver or loon *(Gavia stellata)*. Both nest in northern Europe. On rainy nights divers often lose their bearings and land on a wet road, mistaking it for a river, and because they cannot take off from the ground they are often found there helpless by passers-by.

Certain species of gulls that nest and also winter in large numbers on the shores of Europe, are regular winter visitors to the inland rivers of Europe, though they do this in small numbers. One of the commonest vagrants is the common or mew gull *(Larus canus)*, whose closest breeding grounds are on the coasts of the North and Baltic Seas; another is the herring gull *(Larus argentatus)* and also, though rarely, the lesser black-backed gull *(Larus fuscus)*. The little gull *(Larus minutus)* may also be seen passing through central Europe in large numbers during the spring flight from its winter quarters in the Mediterranean to its nesting grounds in Scandinavia. Other species of gulls may be seen in the interior of Europe only on very rare occasions.

Another rare visitor to inland rivers in winter is the Arctic skua *(Stercorarius parasiticus)*. Other species of Scandinavian water birds are only very occasionally seen in the interior of Europe during winter.

WATER GAME BIRDS

Various water and marshland birds have been hunted for centuries both for their meat and also as a sport (for example heron and crane hunts with trained falcons or other predatory birds). First on the list of water game birds are geese and ducks, which are considered the tastiest. In bygone days geese and ducks were also hunted with falcons or goshawks and this is again becoming a popular sport in certain countries, though not on as large a scale as in medieval times.

Hunting wild geese and ducks must be done prudently for otherwise their numbers might be gravely endangered. In many areas their numbers have dwindled substantially during the past few years. Permission to hunt game birds should be granted only to hunters that show adequate knowledge of the various species so that there is no danger of their shooting rare birds. In recent years certain species such as the goldeneye and red-crested pochard have become established in new areas and these need to be protected if their populations are to grow. Such species may be quite plentiful and therefore are commonly hunted in some countries, but in others they must be protected by law.

The hunting or shooting season varies from country to country. In some places ducks are hunted as early as July, which is not a very good time. The flight feathers of young ducks are not then fully grown, even though they have fledged, and often the birds only flap about or fly just a short distance and with some effort. The victims therefore at this time are generally these young birds and the next generation of strong young individuals cannot thus be guaranteed. It is therefore preferable if the hunting season does not begin until the middle of August, when the young are already as proficient at flying as their elders and the proportion of young and old amongst the downed birds is more balanced.

Ducks are usually hunted on the wing with shotguns using large lead shot. Both males and females are shot in about the same proportion for these birds live in pairs. Shooting birds which are moulting is not only unsportsmanlike but also bad policy from the conservation viewpoint. The males generally moult at a different time from the females and such downed birds are therefore only of one or the other sex. Being paired, their partners are thus left without a mate.

Ducks are generally hunted from a blind in tall reeds on the shores of a pond or lake, in which the hunters conceal themselves. Other hunters ride in boats along the edge of the reed beds and flush the birds, which abruptly fly up and then towards the ambush of the concealed hunters. In this method of hunting it is permitted to shoot only birds on the wing. When hunting waterfowl, of course, hunters must be equipped with dogs trained to retrieve the game from the water, for many of the downed ducks are concealed from sight in the reeds. Ducks are sometimes hunted after sundown when they journey from one pond to another or in search of food. The hunters conceal themselves at the water's edge and wait for the ducks to fly within shooting range. Here, too, it is important to have a well-trained retriever, for many wounded ducks fall into the reeds and are hard to find in the twilight. Hunting after sundown, however, should be forbidden from the conservation viewpoint for that is the time when they fly in search of food and they need peace and quiet to eat their fill.

The protection of ducks and geese in all countries, however, remains a problem. In the main, these are migratory birds and many ducks journey for the winter to other countries than those where they normally nest, which means that in the autumn the hunters often shoot birds that are not local inhabitants. It is during the migration period that ducks and geese are mainly hunted, often without any consideration as to whether they are a common or rare species.

Thankfully, many members of the Anatidae family are extremely shy and wary when migrating. Geese, in particular, gather in large flocks, mainly in open places, with several birds always standing guard so that it is difficult to come within shooting range. Hunters must come under cover of night to the edges of lakes and marshes where wild geese gather, and conceal themselves in previously made camouflaged hides, for there are very few natural hiding places in such locations. At dawn the flocks of geese fly up from the water's surface or small islets and each of the concealed

Fig. 4. A flock of geese in their typical flight formation.

hunters fires several rounds. As a rule, there will be no more geese flying this way. It often happens that the geese bypass them and the hunters wait in vain. At other times a hunter may try to approach a grazing flock until he comes within shooting range, which is even more difficult. The hunter crawls forward on his stomach or has to wade through waist-deep water in a ditch, and when he has finally succeeded in overcoming all the obstacles in his way without

41

attracting the notice of the geese he downs only one or two birds, while the remainder of the flock flies up and away to a safe distance. One may also lie in wait for a flock of geese at dusk when the birds return from their day's feeding to their roosting place. In this case the hunters are also concealed in a blind and it is very important that they refrain from shooting at the first flock to land, for these birds are the most cautious and do not land until they have made

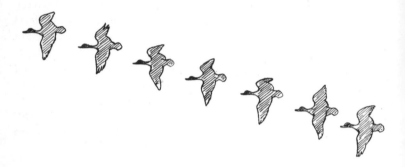

Fig. 5. Ducks in their typical flight formation.

a thorough search of the area, continuing to keep a sharp lookout even afterwards; they often fly off again without landing, returning only after some time. The flocks that follow, however, are not as careful, for they hear and see their fellows on the ground and thus consider it a safe place to land. The flocks descend and land in the immediate vicinity and only then can the hunters begin to fire with success. Another method of hunting geese is from a cart drawn by a horse or ox. It is interesting to note that not only geese but also other species of birds will let a cart pulled by an animal come quite close whereas at the approach of a walking man they will fly off while he is still quite far away. As a rule the carts are camouflaged with dry corn stalks or reeds and several such vehicles can encircle flocks of geese as they feed. This method provides the greatest number of shot birds.

There are, of course, other methods of hunting wild geese, for instance from boats or with decoy geese, when one or more birds which have had their wing feathers trimmed are put out on the water where their honking attracts flocks flying past. In some countries ducks, too, are hunted with decoy birds on smaller ponds where they are within shooting range of the hunters on the shore. Sometimes artificial decoys carved of wood and painted with the appropriate colours are used instead of live birds.

One of the wild geese popularly hunted is the grey lag goose *(Anser anser)*, which may weigh more than five kilograms. It has a discontinuous distribution even in central and western Europe and in Scotland, and occurs in greater numbers in northern Europe. It is one of the largest species of geese and tastes very good.

Another popularly hunted goose is the bean goose *(Anser fabalis)*, weighing up to 4.5 kilograms, which nests in northern Europe and flies in large flocks not only to Europe's western coast but also to many other parts of the Continent. It is generally hunted during its autumn migration flight and is also very tasty.

Other geese favoured by hunters include the lesser white-fronted goose *(Anser erythropus)*, weighing 1.5 to 2.5 kilograms, which also nests in the far northern European tundra and journeys across central Europe to its winter quarters in western and southeastern Europe, and the white-fronted goose *(Anser albifrons)*, which can weigh as much as 3.5 kilograms. It likewise nests in the north European tundra and travels in large flocks across central Europe to its winter quarters on the west European coast. The brent goose *(Branta bernicla)*, nesting beyond the Arctic Circle, the Canada goose *(Branta canadensis)* and the barnacle goose *(Branta leucopsis)*, likewise of the far north, frequently occur on the coast of western Europe and are also occasionally hunted.

Numerous species of duck are widely hunted. Of the non-diving ducks the most important is the mallard, weighing from 0.8 to 1.4 kilograms. It is one of the most plentiful species in all of Europe, and is very tasty. Other species include the gadwall *(Anas strepera)*, the garganey *(Anas querquedula)* and the teal *(Anas crecca)*. Hunting teals, which weigh only 300 to 350 grams, is an exciting sport. These ducks attain speeds of more than sixty miles an hour and it therefore takes an expert marksman to hit such a fast-moving target. Other species of non-diving ducks are more rare but are nevertheless classed as game birds in many countries.

Of the diving ducks the ones most frequently hunted are the pochard *(Aythya ferina)* and tufted duck *(Aythya fuligula)*. Other species of diving ducks are hunted less frequently. When hunting diving ducks it often happens that wounded birds grab hold of a plant with their beak as they fall and will not let go, preferring death by drowning. In such a case even a retriever is of no use.

The coot *(Fulica atra)* is another species much sought after by sportsmen. It is one of the most plentiful of water birds and is found practically everywhere in Europe. In the autumn coots converge in large flocks, often numbering several hundred birds, on ponds and in winter on rivers that do not freeze over. When shot at they generally do not leave a pond but merely fly from one end to another. Coots can be hunted from the shore or from boats, the best time being from the end of August to October. Even though they are not fond of flying, when they do fly their flight is very rapid and shooting one is considered a feat of expert marksmanship. Their meat is quite tasty but it is recommended to cook it with a generous quantity of herbs and spices.

Of the waders found by the waterside the only game bird is the snipe *(Gallinago gallinago)*, one of the commonest of this group of birds. As sportsmen's prizes go, however, it is a very small one, for it weighs only 100 to 160 grams. Hunting snipe is an exciting sport requiring a skilled and experienced marksman, for the bird starts up very suddenly only a few yards in front of the hunter and then flies close above the ground, often following a zig-zag course. Its meat is considered a gastronomic delicacy.

PLATES

Males are marked with the symbol ♂,
females with the symbol ♀.

Great Crested Grebe

Podiceps cristatus

Podicipedidae

The great crested grebe is widespread throughout most of Europe except the northern parts. The populations of northern and eastern Europe are migratory. The great crested grebe inhabits lakes or large ponds with large beds of reeds and rushes. It returns to its nesting grounds sometimes as early as February, though March or April are more usual. An interesting ceremonial courtship takes place on the water preceding nesting. The two partners, separated by a distance of several yards, greet one another by stretching their necks out above the water's surface. Then they swim towards each other, spreading their ruffs, nodding their heads and finally embracing by rubbing their necks, emitting cries throughout. Sometimes they also dive, then surface with water plants in their bills and tread water, facing each other with heads erect. The nest, usually less than eighty centimetres high, is made of various kinds of water plants which the grebes bring up from the depths. After it is completed the female lays three to six eggs which are white at first but then gradually acquire a brown hue. Both partners take turns incubating for a period of twenty-five to twenty-seven days, though the female does the major share of the sitting. After they have dried, the newly hatched nestlings climb up on their parents' backs, concealing themselves under their wings and often being carried about by the adult birds even though capable of swimming and diving by themselves. The parents feed the young small insects, molluscs etc. The diet of adult birds consists mostly of fish and insect larvae.

Length: 48 cm. The 'horns' are absent in the winter plumage. *Voice:* A deep 'kar-arr' or 'er-wick' mainly during the courtship period. *Size of Egg:* 46.5—62.7 ×33.0—39.7 mm.

Little Grebe

Podiceps ruficollis

Podicipedidae

The little grebe inhabits the whole of Europe except the northern parts. Individuals inhabiting eastern Europe are migrant and the populations of central, western and southern Europe are resident. The little grebe is found on lakes and ponds as well as slow-moving water courses with overgrown banks. One may come across it even on very small pools the banks of which are thickly bordered with reeds, rushes, and the like. The little grebe is a remarkably shy bird and remains concealed in the thickets most of the time, venturing forth onto the open water only rarely. The birds arrive at the nesting grounds already paired, the partners often remaining together throughout the winter. The courtship display begins shortly after their arrival. The male puts his head back, ruffles his feathers, pecks at the water and often sends up a spray of water with his feet. He is very tenacious in defending his nesting territory. The little grebe has its first brood in April and a second one in June/July. The nest, consisting of a pile of rotting water plants, is situated directly on the water among reeds. In shallow water it rests on the bottom, in deeper water it is fixed firmly between the reeds. As a rule, the female lays four to six eggs. Both partners share the duties of incubation for a period of twenty to twenty-one days, and both attend upon the young for eight to ten weeks. The diet of the little grebe consists of insects and their larvae, small molluscs, worms, crustaceans, tadpoles, as well as small fish, which it hunts mostly underwater.

Length: 27 cm. The winter plumage is paler on the upperside. *Voice:* A trilling 'whit, whit'. *Size of Egg:* 32.8—43.0 ×23.0—28.3 mm.

Black-necked Grebe

Podiceps nigricollis

Podicipedidae

The black-necked grebe was originally a native of southeastern Europe but during the past eighty years has become widespread throughout western and central Europe as well as in the south of Spain, Italy, England, Holland and eastern France. East European populations are migratory. This species is partial to shallow but large ponds and lakes covered with extensive vegetation in which it hides. Pairs of birds return to the nesting grounds in March/April and begin their courtship display shortly after their arrival. During this performance the partners swim rapidly towards each other, raise their heads erect and shake them. The black-necked grebe is a gregarious bird and stays in groups even when nesting, forming colonies with a great number of nests spaced several yards apart, though they often are more densely clustered. The nest of rotting vegetation is located on the water amongst reeds, rushes, etc., though sometimes it may float freely on the surface at the edge of a reed bed. It is the female that does the actual building of the nest from material brought by the male. The clutch, consisting of three to four and sometimes as many as six eggs, is laid in April/June and both partners share the duties of incubation for nineteen to twenty-three days. The small nestlings are carried about on their parents' backs and cared for by them for a number of weeks. The diet consists of insects and their larvae, small molluscs and crustaceans as well as tadpoles and small fish. The black-necked grebe hunts its prey under water, usually at depths of no more than two metres.

Length: 30 cm.
Voice: Whistling notes that sound like 'poo-eep'.
Size of Egg:
39.0—48.5
×27.1—34.0 mm.

Grey Heron

Ardea cinerea

The grey heron nests in western, central and eastern Europe as well as in the south and along the western coast of Scandinavia, sporadically also in Spain. Western populations are resident, those of more northerly and eastern regions migrate to the Mediterranean in September/October, though one may still see flocks of herons on emptied ponds of central Europe as late as November and beginning of December. When March comes they return to their nesting grounds — overgrown rivers with tree-lined banks, ponds, lakes and swamps, often also woodlands near bodies of water. Their arrival is followed by an interesting courtship display. When the male has acquired a mate the two then build a nest of twigs, sticks, reeds, and the like, usually high up in the tops of both deciduous and coniferous trees. Only rarely is the nest situated among reeds and rushes. There may be several nests on a single tree, often used by the birds several years in succession. In April/May, sometimes even in late March, the female lays four to five eggs which she and her mate take turns incubating for twenty-five to twenty-eight days. The young hatch successively one after the other. At first the parents feed them by putting regurgitated food directly into their beaks, but later they regurgitate it into the nest. At the age of eight to nine weeks the young are already fully grown and capable of flight. The grey heron is a carnivorous bird which captures small fish in shallow water, also tadpoles, frogs, small mammals and small birds, reptiles, molluscs and insects.

Length: 91 cm.
Voice: Numerous croaking and retching notes.
Size of Egg:
52.4—69.5
×38.5—49.7 mm.

Purple Heron

Ardea purpurea

Ardeidae

In Europe the purple heron nests in southern and central France, Spain, Portugal, Italy, the whole of the Balkan Peninsula, Hungary, on rare occasions also in Austria, Czechoslovakia, Switzerland and Holland. European herons are migrant and generally fly to western or eastern Africa for the winter. They return in pairs to their nesting grounds during the month of April and nest in colonies, sometimes in the company of other species of herons. Both partners share the task of building the nest about half a metre above the water's surface. It is usually made of broken reeds or rushes and is added on to and enlarged during the period of incubation. The clutch consists of four to six eggs, which the parents take turns incubating for an average of twenty-six days. Because they begin sitting as soon as the first egg is laid the young do not hatch all at one time but successively, one after the other. The adult birds bring food to the young in their gular pouches and the nestlings take it from their parents' beaks. Later the adult birds regurgitate the food into the nest and the young then take it from there. The nestlings leave the nest at the age of six weeks and are fully independent by the time they are eight weeks old. The purple heron feeds on small fish, frogs and tadpoles as well as lizards and small mammals and on occasion also on young birds. It also captures insects and their larvae, molluscs, worms and other invertebrates. Often the heron wades through shallows or waits motionless until its prey comes close, whereupon it seizes it with a sharp thrust of its beak.

Length: 79 cm.
Voice: Calls that sound like 'rrank'.
Size of Egg:
50.0—61.2
×36.5—44.7 mm.

Night Heron

Ardeidae

Nycticorax nycticorax

The night heron inhabits southern, southeast and southwest Europe, has a discontinuous distribution in central Europe, and also occurs in Holland and in the south of France. Birds that nest on the Continent migrate in autumn to parts as far away as tropical Africa, whence they return again to their nesting grounds in April. Night herons inhabit swamps, lakes, ponds and rivers bordered with trees and thickets. The nest is a haphazard structure of twigs laid on top of each other, and is usually located at a height of one to five metres, in trees sometimes even more than twenty metres above the ground. The work of building is begun by the male, who then tries to attract the partner. When he is joined by a female she then continues the task by herself while the male keeps her supplied with materials. The clutch consists of three to five eggs, which the female begins incubating as soon as the first is laid. The duties of incubation are shared by both partners, the male relieving his mate every two to four hours. The young hatch one after the other within twenty to twenty-three days and are fed in the nest by the adult birds for twenty-one to twenty-eight days. Then they climb out onto the surrounding branches and at the age of six weeks begin to fly about, being fully fledged by the time they are seven to eight weeks old. The diet consists of various fish, insects, worms and the like. Occasionally the night heron will catch a water-newt and even a fieldmouse. It usually forages for food at twilight or before sunrise and spends the day resting in the branches.

Length: 61 cm.
Voice: A cry that sounds like 'guark' and carries a long way.
Size of Egg: 43.7—56.5 ×31.0—39.7 mm.

Little Bittern

Ixobrychus minutus

Ardeidae

All of Europe excepting Scandinavia and the British Isles is the home of the little bittern, though it sometimes makes its way to England, Iceland and Scandinavia, roaming the countryside there before setting out in late August or September for its winter quarters in northwest and east Africa. It sometimes returns to its nesting grounds as early as late March, but April or early May is the more usual time. It inhabits lakes, ponds and river deltas as well as small pools whose shores are covered with thick vegetation. It makes its home in large beds of reeds where it is well concealed, flying up only when disturbed and then quickly hiding again in the vegetation. First to return from the winter quarters is the male, who then selects a suitable site and begins building the nest. A few days later he is joined by the female, who finishes the task with the materials brought her by the male. The structure, made of reed stalks, is very well concealed. The clutch consists of five to six eggs and the female often starts incubating as soon as the first is laid. The male relieves his partner at regular intervals. The young usually hatch after sixteen to nineteen days, remaining in the nest a further ten to twelve days, after which they climb out onto the surrounding vegetation. The parents bring the young food which they regurgitate into the nest during the first few days, later putting it directly into the nestlings' beaks. The little bittern feeds on insects, small fish, tadpoles, molluscs and crustaceans.

Length: 36 cm. The male is black on the back, the female brown. *Voice:* A variety of short, croaking notes. *Size of Egg:* 30.0—39.0 ×23.3—27.7 mm.

Bittern

Ardeidae

Botaurus stellaris

In the warm nights of spring one can hear a frightening, booming note sounding from the swamps and marshes or from vast beds of reeds growing on the edges of ponds and lakes. It is the bittern announcing that it has taken up residence there. The range of occurrence of this robust bird covers all of Europe except the northern parts. In Scandinavia it occurs only in the southern tip and in England it is found only in the southwest parts of the isles. West and south European birds are usually resident, those from other parts often winter in western and southwestern Europe but also in north Africa, leaving their nesting grounds in September/October and returning again in March/April. The flat nest, a pile of reed stalks, is usually located amidst dense vegetation in the shallows and in all probability is built by the female alone. In April/May she lays five to six eggs and begins sitting on them as soon as the first is laid. The male, who may sometimes have several mates, does not help in incubating. The young hatch successively after twenty-five to twenty-seven days and the duty of caring for them also falls to the female, who feeds them food regurgitated into the nest during the first few days. At the age of eight weeks the young are already fully fledged. The bittern often assumes a reed-like pose among the reeds with head erect, its coloration blending perfectly with the surroundings. The mainstay of its diet is insects and their larvae; it also feeds on tadpoles, frogs, small fish and occasionally also small mammals.

Length: 76 cm.
Voice: A deep 'woomp', sometimes also 'aark'.
Size of Egg: 47.5—58.2 ×33.5—41.0 mm.

White Stork

Ciconia ciconia

The white stork is one of the best known of European birds living in the close vicinity of human dwellings and availing itself of man's protection. It nests in central, northwest and southeast Europe and also makes its home in Spain. In Scandinavia it occurs only in the southernmost tip and occasionally wings its way to England and north as far as Norway and Finland. A migrant bird, it leaves its nesting territory any time from early August through September, flying southwest or southeast, depending on the population, as far as east and south Africa. In March or early April it is back again in its nesting grounds, often settling in the very heart of a village, where it builds a large nest in a tree, on a chimney, roof-top, etc. The nest, made of twigs and sticks, is often used for several years and added to every breeding season. A new nest takes about eight days to build. First to arrive at the nesting grounds is the male, the female joining him several days later. The four to five eggs are laid in April/May and both partners share the duties of incubation; however, only the female sits at night. The young usually hatch after thirty to thirty-four days, feeding themselves on food brought them by their parents and regurgitated into the nest. When they are about three weeks old the young storks begin to stand on their feet and at the age of fifty-four to sixty-three days they are already capable of flight. Storks are carnivorous birds, hunting their prey in shallow waters as well as in fields and meadows. They usually feed on small rodents, frogs, lizards, small fish and various invertebrates.

Length: 102 cm.
Voice: Clapping of the bill; the young make mewing sounds.
Size of Egg:
65.0—81.5
×46.0—57.0 mm.

Spoonbill

Platalea leucorodia

Threskiornithidae

The spoonbill breeds in southern Spain, Holland, on the Neusidler Sea, in Hungary and southeast Europe, departing in August/September for its winter quarters in tropical Africa and returning again to its nesting grounds in March/April. After the young have fledged the spoonbill also regularly visits the North Sea coast and occasionally flies as far as Sweden and Norway. The spoonbill inhabits lakes with overgrown shores, river deltas and marshes, being partial to places with bushes and trees. It nests in colonies, often in the company of other species of birds. The nest is made of reeds and rushes on broken and bent reeds, sometimes also of twigs in bushes or even in trees, particularly oaks. It is built by both partners and is often used by the pair for a number of years. The female lays the eggs in May or June. The clutch consists of three to five eggs covered with spots that disappear during incubation. Both partners incubate for twenty-four to twenty-five days and both attend upon the young, which shove their bills down their parents' throats for their food. When they are six to eight weeks old the young birds leave the nest, fledging a short while later. The spoonbill flies fairly rapidly with neck stretched straight out in front, now and then gliding through the air with motionless wings. The bird's diet consists of various water insects and their larvae, also frogs' eggs, crustaceans, small fish, and the like. The spoonbill catches its prey by swinging its wide, partly immersed bill from side to side as it wades through the water.

Length: 86 cm. During the breeding season it has a crest on the head.
Voice: Deep, hoarse notes and also clapping of the bill.
Size of Egg: 52.7—74.6 ×36.8—49.5 mm.

Mallard or Wild Duck

Anas platyrhynchos

Anatidae

The mallard is one of the commonest and most widely distributed species of duck. It nests throughout the whole of Europe, where it is either resident or dispersive, and in the northernmost areas a migrant to winter quarters in central and western Europe or in the Mediterranean. It returns to its nesting grounds in pairs at the end of February or in early March, the males having selected their mates during the autumn or winter months. The mallard inhabits still waters and sometimes also rivers — even in towns. Spring is the time of courtship, when the partners swim around each other, the male lowers his bill and ruffles his feathers, twitches his tail, nods his head, then plunges his bill into the water, and so forth. The nesting site is selected by the drake but the nest is built by the duck. It is usually located on the ground, often some distance inland; also in trees in nests abandoned by other birds as well as in holes. It is lined with leaves, plant stalks, small twigs, etc. gathered in the immediate vicinity, and furthermore covered with a layer of down. Before leaving the nest the duck carefully covers the eggs with down. There are usually nine to thirteen eggs, which the duck incubates alone for a period of twenty-two to twenty-six days. When the young ducklings' feathers have dried she takes them out to the water. Mallards forage for food after dusk. They feed on various seeds, plant shoots and grass and also collect food on the water's surface, hunt insects, worms, etc. The young ducklings' diet consists in large part of insects, crustaceans, molluscs as well as green plant parts.

Length: Male 57 cm, female 49 cm. Marked sexual dimorphism. The male's non-breeding plumage resembles that of the female. *Voice:* The male's note is a whistling 'yeeb', the female quacks loudly. *Size of Egg:* 50.0—65.0 ×37.0—45.8 mm.

Teal

Anatidae

Anas crecca

The teal, weighing only about 300 grams, is the smallest of European ducks. Its range of distribution includes all of Europe, the only places where it does not nest being Spain, Portugal, Italy and the Balkans, though it occurs there in plenty during the winter months when these areas are visited by populations from Scandinavia and northeastern Europe. West European populations are resident. Some birds even fly to Africa — as far as the Sudan. The teal returns to its breeding grounds in March or early April, seeking out inland stretches of water bordered with thick vegetation and with meadows nearby. The birds arrive at the nesting site already in pairs formed in their winter quarters in February/ March. The nest is built by the female on the ground in tall grass, clumps of grass, as well as beneath a thick willow or alder bush, and may be some distance from water. It is lined with dry vegetation, stalks, leaves, etc., and edged with down. Between mid-April and beginning of June the female begins incubating the eight to ten eggs, sitting on them alone for twenty-two to twenty-five days. During this time the male swims in the water close to the nest. The ducklings are small but very agile, and able to dive and gather food by themselves. They begin to fly at the age of one month. The teal's diet consists of vegetable matter and animal food, the latter being the mainstay in spring and summer whereas in autumn it feeds on seeds and plant parts. The young feed on small invertebrates as well as green plant parts. When the young have fledged the birds form large flocks.

Length: Male 36 cm, female 34 cm. Sexual dimorphism. *Voice:* The male's note is a ringing 'krrit', the female utters a rapid, harsh quack. *Size of Egg:* 41.0—50.0 ×30.0—35.5 mm.

Garganey

Anatidae

Anas querquedula

The garganey inhabits western, central, eastern and northeastern Europe. In England it occurs only in the southeast and in Scandinavia also only on the eastern coast. Birds from central and eastern Europe migrate in August-November to Africa, wintering mostly in the tropical areas. West European populations winter also in Spain. The garganey is plentiful in places but it never forms as large flocks as its relative the teal. It inhabits marshy and swampy sites as well as lakes and ponds bordered with thick vegetation, being partial to places with meadows nearby. The birds arrive at their nesting grounds in late March or April, usually already in pairs; as a rule, several pairs participate jointly in the courtship antics, swimming in a circle, the males with ruffled feathers close behind their partners, heads bent and bills immersed in the water. The males nod their heads up and down, occasionally bending them backward, and complete the display by flying rapidly in small groups close above the water's surface. In late April, May or June the female builds the nest in a shallow depression in the ground, lining it with fine plant parts. She alone incubates the eight to eleven eggs for twenty-one to twenty-five days and also attends the young unaided by her mate. The diet of these ducks consists of seeds, green plant parts, insects and their larvae, worms, molluscs, spiders and on occasion also small fish and tadpoles. Garganeys are among the fastest fliers in the bird realm, attaining speeds of more than sixty miles per hour.

Length: Male 40 cm, female 36 cm, weight ca. 350 g. Sexual dimorphism.
Voice: The male utters a rattling noise, the female quacks.
Size of Egg: 39.3—50.1 ×29.7—35.5 mm.

Gadwall

Anas strepera

Anatidae

The gadwall is a common duck of eastern Europe and the eastern part of central Europe and is also found in northwestern Europe, Great Britain and the south of Sweden, in rare instances also in southern Spain and France. West European populations are resident, the others are migrant, wintering mostly in southwestern Europe as well as in Africa as far as Ethiopia. They leave their breeding grounds in September to November. Late March or April is the time when the gadwall returns to its nesting territory, mostly inland bodies of stagnant water bordered with thick vegetation. The birds are already paired when they arrive but it is interesting to note that during the courtship display one female is surrounded by several males. The males perform a sort of courtship flight during which they cease flapping their wings and plummet in a slanting line to the ground. The nest is placed on the ground, usually on small islets, banks, etc., near water. It is generally well concealed in grass and is lined with bits of dry plants. In May or June it contains a clutch of seven to twelve eggs, which the female incubates alone for twenty-six to twenty-seven days. As soon as the newly hatched ducklings have dried she leads them to the water. The young fledge at the age of seven weeks, after which they roam the countryside until the time comes to leave for their winter quarters. The gadwall's diet consists of plant parts and seeds; only occasionally does it feed also on molluscs and water insects. The young, however, consume animal food in plenty.

Length: Male 51 cm, female 48 cm. Sexual dimorphism. *Voice:* The male utters whistling notes; the female's cry sounds like 'kaaak-kaaak-kak-kak-kak'. *Size of Egg:* 50.3—59.9 ×34.5—43.5 mm.

Wigeon

Anas penelope

The wigeon inhabits north and northeast Europe and also nests in Scotland and on the shores of the Baltic Sea. In Scotland, Iceland and on Scandinavia's southwest coast it is resident or else roams the countryside in winter. Birds inhabiting other parts of Europe migrate southwest, wintering on the North Sea coast and southern shore of the Baltic Sea, in great numbers also on the west European coast and in the Mediterranean countries and sometimes even as far away as Africa on the lakes of Nigeria. Occasionally it winters on the rivers of central Europe. It leaves its nesting grounds at the end of August or in September, returning again in March or early April, arriving there already in pairs. The wigeon is found on inland stretches of stagnant water of all kinds as long as they are bordered by thick vegetation. The nest, made of dry plant partsl ined with a layer of grey down, is built by the female on the ground, generally close to the water and concealed by tall plants or a bush. The seven to ten eggs are incubated by the duck alone for twenty-two to twenty-three days, on rare occasions as much as twenty-five days. When the newly hatched ducklings have dried their mother leads them to the water, where they are joined by the drake. The wigeon's diet consists mainly of the green parts of plants growing in water as well as on land, seeds and shoots etc., though it also sometimes feeds on animal food such as insects and their larvae, spiders, molluscs, worms, etc. Young ducklings feed mainly on small invertebrates.

Length:
Male 49 cm, female 44 cm. Sexual dimorphism.
Voice: The male utters whistling notes that sound like 'whee-oo', the female a low, purring note.
Size of Egg:
49.2—59.9 ×34.7—42.1 mm.

Pintail

Anatidae

Anas acuta

The pintail makes its home mostly in northern and northeastern Europe, though it is also found in the eastern and northern parts of central Europe, in northwestern Europe and in England. In England and northwest Europe it is partly resident whereas birds inhabiting other parts of Europe are migrant and winter in western Europe, the Mediterranean and Africa as far as the Sudan, mostly in the upper reaches of the Nile. The pintail leaves for its winter quarters in August/September, returning again to its nesting grounds at the end of March and in April. It favours large expanses of still water, chiefly lakes, and in the north is found in abundance also in the tundra, though it also occurs in marshy areas and often near the sea. In Scandinavia it is one of the commonest of ducks. The birds arrive at their nesting grounds in spring already in pairs formed in their winter quarters or during the return journey in spring. The nest is fashioned by the female in a depression in the ground lined with dry plant parts gathered in the immediate vicinity. It is concealed in a clump of grass or in thickets by the waterside, though it may also be located in a meadow or even in woodland, often several hundred yards from water. The seven to eleven eggs are incubated twenty-two to twenty-three days by the female alone while the male keeps guard close by, well concealed in the grass but keeping a sharp lookout with his head raised. The pintail feeds on various seeds, shoots, green plant parts, etc. as well as on insects and their larvae, spiders, molluscs, worms and occasionally a tadpole or small frog.

Length:
Male 70.5 cm,
female 57.5 cm.
Sexual
dimorphism.
Voice: The male
utters a low
whistle,
the female
a low
quack.
Size of Egg:
44.1—61.9
×33.9—43.0 mm.

Shoveler

Anas clypeata

Anatidae

The shoveler nests in east, northeast, central and western Europe. In Scandinavia it occurs only in the southern parts of Sweden and Finland and on the eastern coast of Iceland. In western Europe it is resident or else roams the countryside, whereas birds inhabiting the other parts of the Continent are migrants, wintering sometimes in western Europe but mostly in the Mediterranean or in Africa as far as Uganda and Ghana. The shoveler departs for its winter quarters in late August and September, returning to its nesting grounds again at the end of March or in April. It nests on inland lakes and ponds, even smaller ones, with an open expanse of water as well as in shallow waters bordered with thick vegetation. It is partial to bodies of water adjoining large meadows. In May/June the female prepares the nest in a depression in the ground in grass, often in a meadow some distance from the water, lining it with dry plant parts. When the clutch is complete, i.e. seven to twelve eggs, she lines and borders the nest with a large quantity of grey pale-spotted down and then incubates the eggs alone for twenty-three to twenty-five days, though this period may be as little as twenty-one and as much as twenty-seven days. After the ducklings have hatched she takes them to shallow water where they easily find food. At the age of six weeks the ducklings are already able to fly. The diet consists of various crustaceans, insect larvae, molluscs and worms as well as plankton and bits of water plants which the bird sieves with its bill. In the autumn it also gathers various seeds.

Length: Male 51.5 cm, female 47.5 cm. Sexual dimorphism. *Voice:* The male's note is a deep 'tuk-tuk', the female's sounds like 'woak', however, they are heard only infrequently. *Size of Egg:* 47.1—58.0 ×34.5—40.0 mm.

Red-crested Pochard

Netta rufina

The range of this diving duck, the red-crested pochard, covers southeastern Spain, southeastern France, the Mediterranean islands, part of northwestern Europe, Holland and Belgium; it also has an interrupted distribution in central Europe, where it has become more widespread during the past several years. It is also found in parts of southeastern Europe and occasionally occurs as a dispersive in England and farther north in Sweden, though it does not nest there. Birds inhabiting the Mediterranean region are resident, those from other areas migrate in October—December to the Mediterranean for the winter. In late March or in April they return again to their nesting grounds on deep, calm stretches of water or slow-flowing water courses with ample vegetation. In steppe regions the red-crested pochard also inhabits salt lakes. In May/June the female builds the nest amidst vegetation or in thickets on the the ground, sometimes, however, also in reed-beds on bent reeds. It is generally lined with dry plant bits as well as small twigs and sometimes even green leaves. It also contains a large quantity of buff-grey down. As a rule the clutch consists of six to ten eggs, which the female incubates alone for twenty-six to twenty-eight days. The red-crested pochard forages for food on the surface of the water but sometimes dives for it, being able to descend to depths of two to four metres. The diet consists of various water plants and seeds, small crustaceans, molluscs, worms and insects.

Length: Male 57 cm, female 51 cm. Sexual dimorphism. *Voice:* The male's is a thin, hoarse note, the female's a quacking or rasping sound. *Size of Egg:* 51.7—62.3 ×38.2—45.1 mm.

Tufted Duck

Aythya fuligula

Anatidae

The tufted duck was originally a native of north and northeast Europe, whence it spread to west and central Europe, where it is now in many places one of the commonest of ducks. The populations of west and northwest Europe are resident, those of other parts are migrant. Scandinavian populations often winter in central Europe on large rivers that do not freeze over, even in large cities, but the tufted duck's main winter quarters are the shores of western Europe, particularly the coast of England and the Mediterranean. The birds return to their breeding grounds from mid-March to April, settling on stagnant water, on lakes and ponds as well as slow-flowing water courses bordered with thick vegetation. They are partial to stretches of water with small islets on which they are fond of building their nests. This task is performed by the female in May — July. The nest is a small hollow in the ground near water. The six to twelve eggs are incubated by the duck alone, usually for a period of twenty-four to twenty-six days. About twelve hours after they have hatched, the young black-coloured ducklings are led out onto the water by the duck. At the age of seven weeks they are already capable of flight. The diet consists mostly of animal food — crustaceans, molluscs, insects and their larvae and other invertebrates. It also feeds on vegetable matter, seeds, pieces of water plants, etc. It dives to depths of two to three metres for its food but is capable of diving to depths of fourteen metres.

Length: Male 42 cm, female 38 cm. Sexual dimorphism. *Voice:* The female has a hoarse 'arrr', the male a soft, whistling courtship note. *Size of Egg:* 53.0—67.1 ×37.7—47.2 mm.

Pochard

Anatidae

Aythya ferina

The pochard is a very common diving duck with a widespread distribution embracing all of eastern, central and northwestern Europe and England. In Scandinavia it occurs only in the eastern parts of Sweden and Finland and in the southernmost part of Norway. In mild climates it is resident or dispersive, whereas birds inhabiting northern and eastern Europe winter in the Mediterranean, sometimes also in central Europe, where they form flocks on large rivers and lakes that do not freeze over. September to mid-November is the period when they depart for their winter quarters, returning again to their nesting grounds from mid-March to early April. Their favourite haunts are inland lakes and ponds, even smaller ones, bordered by thick vegetation. The birds pair in their winter quarters but arrive at the breeding grounds in flocks. The nest is built by the female on the ground amidst vegetation near the water, often on islets, thick clumps of grass, etc. The hollow is fairly deep and lined with bits of green plants and thick dark-coloured down. The clutch consists of five to eleven eggs, which the duck incubates alone for twenty-three to twenty-six days. The young ducklings are led out on the water by the duck the very day they hatch. The diet consists of the green parts of aquatic vegetation as well as seeds. Plant food predominates; the young, however, and on occasion also the adults, likewise feed on crustaceans, molluscs, insects and their larvae, other invertebrates and sometimes also small tadpoles. They dive for their food to depths of 1.5 to 2.5 metres.

Length:
Male 46 cm,
female 42 cm.
Sexual
dimorphism.
Weight
about 1 kg.
Voice: The male's
consists of
whistling notes,
the female's is
a harsh,
growling noise.
Size of Egg:
55.8—68.5
×39.0—46.9 mm.

♀

♂

Ferruginous Duck

Aythya nyroca

Anatidae

The ferruginous duck inhabits southern and southeast Europe and also occurs in southern Spain. One sometimes comes across it also in central Europe and the south of France. It is resident in the Mediterranean region but birds from other parts leave their nesting grounds for the Mediterranean in winter. Occasionally the ferruginous duck occurs as a dispersive in England and Scandinavia. It never forms large flocks but usually can be seen in pairs or small groups and arrives at its nesting grounds in pairs in late March or April. The birds select calm bodies of water overgrown with vegetation but with a small expanse of open water. The nest is built by the female on the ground in dense grass and reeds near the water. Sometimes, however, it may also be built on a pile of bent reeds, on a floating clump of grass, etc. It is lined with various parts of green plants from the immediate neighbourhood but these soon dry out. The down with which the duck borders the nest is brownish-grey with paler tips and centre. The eggs, usually six to twelve, are laid in May/June and incubated by the female alone for a period of twenty-five to twenty-eight days, the male remaining close by during the first few days. The day after hatching the young ducklings are already briskly diving and swimming in the water. At the age of eight weeks they are already capable of flight. The diet consists primarily of plant food, which the ducks gather mostly underwater. They also hunt small invertebrates such as insects, crustaceans, molluscs, etc.

Length:
Male 42 cm, female 40 cm. Sexual dimorphism.
Voice:
An oft-repeated note that sounds like 'grrr grrr'.
Size of Egg:
47.2—62.8 ×33.7—43.0 mm.

Grey Lag Goose

Anser anser

Anatidae

The grey lag goose makes its home in Scotland, Iceland, and on the shores of Scandinavia as well as in parts of central and southeast Europe. The birds of Scotland are resident, those inhabiting northern and central Europe winter in western Europe and the Mediterranean, leaving their nesting grounds in September/October and returning again in March. Sites selected for their nests are large, calm expanses of water, lakes and ponds with old reed beds, above all places with extensive meadows nearby, also swampy sites, small islets by the seashore, flooded riverine woodlands, etc. Grey lag geese pair for life. On their return from their winter quarters they usually establish themselves in the same nesting territory. The nest, built by the female alone, may be located on dry ground as well as on water on piles of old bent reeds and even in the tops of small, old willows. Nests on islets may be located in quite open situations. The material of which the nest is made is gathered in the immediate vicinity. The edge is lined with a thick layer of down. As a rule the goose lays four to nine eggs, which she incubates alone for twenty-seven to thirty days while the gander keeps guard close by. Both parents care for the newly hatched goslings. The goslings are capable of flight at the age of fifty-seven days but remain in the company of their parents, the individual families then joining to form large flocks. The diet of the grey lag goose consists mostly of the green parts of plants and various seeds. The young goslings feed themselves, nibbling fine green leaves at first.

Length:
Male 82.5 cm, female 70.5 cm. The male and female have like plumage.
Voice: The familiar call 'aahng-ung-ung'.
Size of Egg: 74.0—99.0 ×51.4—62.0 mm.

Mute Swan

Anatidae

Cygnus olor

The range of occurrence of the mute swan covers England, northwest and central Europe, southern Sweden and southeast Europe, namely around the northern coast of the Black Sea and round the Caspian Sea. In most parts of its range it is resident, though it roams the countryside in winter, seeking larger rivers and bodies of water that do not freeze over. More northerly populations are migrant and winter on the shores of the Baltic or fly as far as Belgium and Holland. The mute swan usually returns to its nesting grounds in late March or in April, seeking out lakes and large ponds bordered with reeds and other vegetation and settling also in river deltas. The birds arrive already paired, usually remaining with one partner for life. However, if one of them dies the other soon finds a new mate. The large nest is built by the female in beds of reeds or rushes. She is aided in her task by the male, who brings her material from the neighbourhood. The four to seven eggs are incubated mostly by the female. Occasionally she is relieved by the male for a short while but otherwise he remains in the immediate vicinity keeping guard and attacking all intruders. The young generally hatch after thirty-five days and are cared for by both parents. They do not fledge until they are four-and-a-half months old and attain full maturity at the age of four years. The diet consists mostly of vegetable matter, though the mute swan feeds partly also on animal food — insects, crustaceans, water-newts, tadpoles and small fish.

Length:
Male 169 cm,
female 155 cm.
Weight 10 kg.
The male
and female have
like plumage.
Voice: A hissing
sound.
Size of Egg:
98.8—122.0
×68.0—80.0 mm.

Red Kite

Milvus milvus

Widespread in the warmer parts of Europe is the handsome predator, the red kite, found in Spain, Italy and southeast Europe, also in France, central Europe and the western parts of eastern Europe, as well as Wales and southern Sweden. As late as the fifteenth and sixteenth centuries it was still one of the commonest London birds but then became extinct in the whole of Britain except for a small part of south Wales. In southern regions it is quite plentiful in places, in more northerly parts, however, it is a rare bird. In Wales and the Mediterranean it is resident, whereas birds inhabiting other parts of Europe leave at the end of August or in September to winter in southern Europe and north Africa. Migrants form flocks of fifty to two hundred birds which hunt jointly and roost together in woodlands. The nest is built in April or May, usually in the highest trees on the margins of woods close to meadows. The structure, measuring one metre across, is made of sticks and twigs, and lined with straw, rags and pieces of paper, etc. Often, however, the red kite will settle in an abandoned nest of some other raptor or even a heron. The female lays two to four eggs, which she incubates mostly alone for twenty-eight to thirty days. Only sometimes is she assisted by the male. The young remain in the nest for forty to fifty-four days, during which time the parents keep them constantly supplied with food. The red kite feeds on various invertebrates and smaller vertebrates, catching frogs, lizards, rodents and smaller birds not adept at flying, also the occasional fish and bits of carrion.

Length: 62 cm.
Wingspan:
145 to 155 cm.
The male and female have like plumage.
Voice:
A trilling
'hi-hi-heea'.
Size of Egg:
51.5—63.0
×40.2—49.0 mm.

94

Black Kite

Accipitridae

Milvus migrans

Rising and falling in graceful undulating flight the black kite may be seen winging its way over the surface of a pond, lake or river in almost any part of Europe excepting the west coast, England and Scandinavia. Only rarely does it nest in central Europe, birds seen here usually being visitors on their migratory flight south. In southerly areas, however, it is quite plentiful. August and September are the time of departure for its winter quarters in Africa and March is the month of its return to its nesting grounds. It inhabits lowland, broadleaved, coniferous as well as mixed woodlands, usually nesting in sites close to stagnant or flowing water. It is often found in colonies of herons, cormorants and other fish-eating birds where it has access to ample fish remnants. In spring, paired birds perform courtship flights high up in the air. The nest, built in trees five to twenty-five metres above the ground, is a haphazard structure of sticks and twigs. Frequently the black kite will take over the abandoned nest of a stork, heron, and the like. Sometimes it nests in colonies. The two to three eggs are incubated for twenty-eight days by the female, relieved now and then by the male. The young fledge at the age of forty-two to forty-five days. The diet consists of carrion, fish remnants and dead nestlings in colonies of herons, etc. The black kite is fond of gathering animal remnants on the water's surface, above which it hovers motionless in a single spot. It also hunts frogs and small mammals, which it feeds to its offspring. On fledging the birds form large flocks.

Length: 57 cm.
Wingspan:
114 to 118 cm.
The male and female have like plumage.
Voice:
A trilling 'hihihihee'.
Size of Egg:
46.0—61.0
×37.0—46.5 mm.

Marsh Harrier

Circus aeruginosus

Accipitridae

The marsh harrier, a brownish raptorial bird, may be seen gliding skilfully close above the vast beds of reeds where it nests, be it in lake or pond country. One may also come across it in marshes and even in fields close to water in southern Europe. Its range covers almost all of Europe; in Scandinavia, however, it inhabits only southern Sweden and in England only the southeastern parts. It also occurs as an occasional dispersive in Ireland and Norway. Birds inhabiting central and eastern Europe leave in August or the beginning of September for Africa or the Middle East, whereas those of southern and western Europe are resident, roaming the countryside in winter. In late March to mid-April the marsh harrier returns to its nesting grounds and in May or June builds a nest of twigs, aquatic vegetation, etc. among reeds. The female generally lays three to six eggs, which she incubates alone for thirty to thirty-three, and sometimes as much as thirty-seven days. During this period the male brings her food to the nest. When the young have hatched he also brings food for them, passing it to the female, who then feeds them. When they are older she, too, forages for food to supply their needs. The young are capable of flight at the age of forty to fifty days though they often venture forth from the nest before that. The marsh harrier's diet consists of small mammals and birds, occasionally also fish, frogs, and sometimes even birds' eggs and insects. As a rule it does not attack ducks, which take practically no notice of this raptorial bird in flight.

Length: 52 cm.
Wingspan:
116 to 126 cm.
The male's head
is greyish-ochre.
Voice: The male's
during courtship
is a ringing
'quee-a',
the female's
a whistling
'hieeeeh'.
Size of Egg:
43.0—56.0
×34.5—44.5 mm.

Hen Harrier

Circus cyaneus

The hen harrier, one of the handsomest of raptorial birds, inhabits almost all of Europe, though it is absent in parts. It nests, for example, only in northern England and southwest Ireland, in Sweden only in the northeast, in Spain and Italy only in the northern parts. North and east European populations are migrant, leaving at the end of August for their winter quarters in the Mediterranean and North Africa. Birds inhabiting other parts of Europe are resident though some also migrate south. The hen harrier inhabits open country with spreading meadows, bogs and swamps as well as steppes. In Europe it is partial to vast marshes. In April it returns to its breeding territory, commencing its striking aerial courtship acrobatics soon after its arrival. In April/May the two partners build a nest on the ground, usually by a swamp, in heather, also in stands of grain or maize, in the grass of a clearing, etc. It is fairly small and made of twigs, reeds and grass. The female lays three to five, sometimes, though rarely, as many as eight eggs, which she incubates alone for twenty-nine to thirty days. The male brings her food during this period and later also for the young nestlings, passing it to the female who divides it up amongst her offspring. The nestlings begin to try their wings at the age of thirty-five to forty-two days. The hen harrier's diet consists mostly of small mammals such as dormice and mice. On occasion it will capture a rabbit, small hare or bird as large as a pheasant. As a rule it hunts on the ground. It never perches in trees.

Length: 47 cm.
Wingspan:
103 to 108 cm.
Sexual
dimorphism.
Voice: During
the courtship
flight the male's
note sounds like
'ke-ke-ke', the
female's is
a high-pitched
'pee-e'.
Size of Egg:
39.3—52.1
×31.0—40.0 mm.

Montagu's Harrier

Circus pygargus

Accipitridae

Montagu's harrier is widespread but not very plentiful in western, southern, central and eastern Europe. It is not found in Ireland and in Sweden occurs only rarely in the south. A migrant, it leaves its nesting grounds in August or September for tropical and South Africa, returning again at the end of April or beginning of May. It inhabits marshy meadows, dry bogs, and also larger beds of reeds, etc. The striking courtship flights begin shortly after the birds' arrival and then they soon set about building the nest. Located on the ground, often in a very damp spot on the edge of a reed bed, in a swamp, etc., it is made of small twigs, reeds and the like and lined with fine vegetation. The female usually lays four to five eggs at intervals of thirty-six hours to three days, which she incubates alone for twenty-eight to twenty-nine days, beginning as soon as the first is laid. The young, therefore, especially if there are a greater number, show marked differences in size and the youngest often does not survive the competition of the elder and stronger brothers and sisters. The male brings food to the female on the nest as well as to the young during the first weeks, cleaning it partially before passing it to the female who feeds it to the nestlings. When they are three weeks old she, too, leaves the nest in search of food. When the nestlings are capable of tearing the prey themselves then the male gives it to them directly. The diet consists of small mammals as well as lizards and birds' eggs. Sometimes Montagu's harrier also hunts smaller birds and larger insects such as locusts.

Length: 42.5 cm.
Wingspan: 109 cm.
Sexual dimorphism.
Voice: Like that of the hen harrier, in gliding flight also 'kek-kek-kek'.
Size of Egg: 36.0—47.2 ×29.5—35.7 mm. The eggs are all white, only rarely speckled.

Osprey or Fish Hawk

Accipitridae

Pandion haliaetus

This handsome raptor inhabits northern and eastern Europe, occasionally also the north-eastern parts of central Europe, and is likewise found in Scotland and on the southern coast of Spain. The osprey is a migrant, leaving its nesting grounds in August or September for its winter quarters in tropical and South Africa. Its favourite haunts are large freshwater lakes and ponds though it is also found on the seashore. On returning to its breeding grounds in April or early May it sets about building a nest, usually in a tall tree. It is made of very thick, dry branches without bark. The female lays two to four eggs in April or May and incubates them for thirty-five to thirty-six days. Sometimes she is relieved by the male, who otherwise brings her food, which he places on the edge of the nest. He also brings food for the nestlings, during the first few weeks by himself, later being joined in his quest by the female. The young leave the nest after fifty-one to seventy days but continue to be fed by the parents a whole month longer. The osprey feeds mainly on fish, being excellently equipped for grasping its prey in having long-clawed toes that are reversible so that they can be positioned opposite each other — two in front and two behind. When searching for food the osprey flies above the water's surface at a height of about twenty-five metres, often hovering a while in a single spot. On sighting its prey it plunges into the water with such speed that it often vanishes below the surface. Grasping the prey in its claws it flies to a nearby tree before eating it.

Length: 55 cm.
Wingspan:
155 to 170 cm.
The male
and female have
like plumage.
Voice: A short,
cheeping
whistle.
Size of Egg:
50.4—69.0
×40.2—52.0 mm.

Red-footed Falcon

Falco vespertinus

The red-footed falcon, a handsome raptorial bird of the falcon tribe, is widespread in east and southeast Europe as well as in the eastern part of central Europe. During the migratory period it visits England, France, Spain and the more southerly parts of central Europe. It is a migrant and at the end of August or beginning of September it sets out on its journey to its winter quarters in tropical and South Africa, returning again to its nesting grounds in flat country in the vicinity of water in April or early May. Red-footed falcons are gregarious birds and usually nest in colonies. Often they seek out the nesting grounds of rooks and occupy their old abandoned nests. In May or June, occasionally sometimes also in July, the female lays four to five eggs, which she and her partner take turns incubating for some twenty-eight days. The newly hatched nestlings are fed by the female with food brought by the male, though when they are larger he also feeds them himself. The young falcons leave the nest after twenty-eight to thirty days but continue to be fed by the parents a short while longer. After fledging whole families roam the countryside until the time for their southward journey, when they join to form large flocks. Groups numbering as many as several thousands of birds have been observed in some places in the autumn. The mainstay of the diet is insects. Red-footed falcons are fond of banding together in large groups to capture beetles, butterflies, etc. on the surface of stagnant and flowing water. They will also capture swarming ants.

Length:
Male 28 cm,
female 30 cm.
Wingspan:
70 to 72 cm.
Sexual
dimorphism.
Voice: A note
that resembles
the wryneck's
and sounds like
'kikikiki'.
Size of Egg:
30.7—42.0
×26.3—32.5 mm.

♀

♂

Crane

Gruidae

Grus grus

The large crane is today found only in north and northeast Europe and the northern parts of central Europe. At one time it was very plentiful throughout central and western Europe but civilization caused its reduction. Cranes migrate as far as the Sudan and Ethiopia but some winter also in the Mediterranean. They leave their breeding grounds in September/October, returning again from the middle of March to April. They inhabit marshy areas with lakes, extensive meadows near large ponds and lakes, swamp areas and also marshy woodlands next to meadows. The birds pair after returning to their nesting grounds, each pair choosing and fiercely defending their own territory. The courtship antics are striking and vociferous. During the performance the cranes utter loud trumpet-like calls, leap high in the air and spread their wings, hop on one foot and run around in circles; in short they do a sort of dance. The nest of reeds and twigs is built on small flat islets, also on broken and bent reeds in swamps, on clumps of grass, and often in the same spot for a number of years. In dry locations the nest is low, in swamps it is high and broad. In April or May the female generally lays two, sometimes one or three eggs, which she and her partner take turns incubating for twenty-eight to thirty-one days. On hatching, the young cranes, which have a short bill at first, scamper about the neighbourhood; they are also able to swim. The crane feeds on seeds, grain, green plant parts, insects, molluscs, etc., and occasionally also captures small vertebrates.

Length:
Male 122 cm, female 112 cm. The male and female have like plumage.
Wingspan: About 220 cm.
Voice: Loud trumpet-like calls, in the vicinity of the nest cries that sound like 'kr-r-r'.
Size of Egg: 85.0—109.0 ×56.0—67.0 mm.

Water Rail

Rallidae

Rallus aquaticus

The water rail inhabits all of Europe except the northernmost parts. In Scandinavia it occurs only in the south, but it nests also in Iceland. Birds inhabiting western and southern Europe are resident, those from other parts migrate in September/October, usually wintering in the Mediterranean region; in mild winters, however, eastern populations may go no farther than central Europe. In March/April they appear again in their nesting grounds — thick vegetation bordering lakes and ponds as well as bogs, marshes, and the like. The nest of dry as well as green plant parts is built by the partners in a well concealed spot in thick clumps of grass, reeds, etc. In April/May the female generally lays six to twelve, sometimes sixteen eggs, which she and her partner take turns incubating for nineteen to twenty-one days. In June/July the two birds build a new nest and have a second brood. The newly hatched nestlings are black and very agile; as soon as they have dried they scatter in the reeds amongst which they move with great adroitness. When they are hungry they utter soft peeps to attract the notice of their parents who bring them food, which the young take from their beaks. They eat insects and their larvae, molluscs, spiders, also green plant parts and in the autumn various small seeds. The water rail is on the move mostly at twilight and at night, sleeping in a well concealed spot during the day. When it walks it holds its neck stretched forward, jerking it as it goes along. It can swim and is even known to dive. In the autumn it forages for food at the edge of reed beds.

Length: 28 cm. The male and female have like plumage. *Voice:* 'Krruih', an oft-repeated 'pit', during the courtship display 'gep-gep-gep' followed by a ringing 'krui, krui, krui' and 'kik, kik, kik'. *Size of Egg:* 31.9—40.0 ×23.5—27.6 mm.

Spotted Crake

Porzana porzana

The spotted crake nests in practically all of Europe excepting the northernmost parts. It is absent in Spain, Portugal and Ireland. In September/October it leaves its nesting grounds, wintering in southwestern Europe and the Mediterranean but mostly in northwest and east Africa, thousands of these birds staying in the region of the Upper Nile. When migrating it flies by night. The spotted crake inhabits lakes and ponds bordered with thick vegetation, marshes and swamps as well as the banks of slow-moving water courses, primarily overgrown river deltas. It returns to its breeding grounds in mid-April, and in May or June, sometimes at the end of April, builds the nest, later building a second one in June/July. The structure is made of both dry and green leaves of reeds, rushes and the like and is well concealed in reeds. The clutch usually comprises eight to twelve eggs, which the partners take turns incubating for eighteen to twenty-one days. The young remain in the nest for one or two days and then scamper about in the vicinity amidst the thick vegetation. The parents bring them food in their bills. This usually consists of insects and their larvae, worms and spiders. However, the spotted crake also feeds on small molluscs, centipedes and other invertebrates as well as the green leaves of duckweed and in the autumn small seeds. The adult birds sometimes still bring the young food when the female is already preparing to have a second brood. Even after these have hatched the young birds of the first brood remain near their parents.

Length: 23 cm. The male and female have like plumage.
Voice: During the nesting period a whistling 'whitt', especially in the evening and at night.
Size of Egg: 29.1—37.5 ×21.7—26.8 mm.

Moorhen

Gallinula chloropus

Rallidae

The moorhen is widely distributed throughout the whole of Europe except the northernmost parts. Inhabitants of the eastern and northern parts of Europe are migrants whereas those of other parts remain in their nesting grounds for the winter, though sometimes they, too, leave, e.g. flying from central Europe to western Europe and the Mediterranean. The moorhen returns to its breeding grounds often as early as the middle of March. It inhabits ponds, lakes and slow-flowing water courses bordered with thick vegetation. It may be found even on quite small ponds and pools if they are bordered with thick reed beds. When swimming it continually flips its tail. The nest, located in rushes, reeds or clumps of grass, is made of dry reeds, rushes and the like by both partners. Each pair has its own nesting territory, which both birds fiercely defend. They have one brood in April or May, a second in June or July, and sometimes a third one in August. The female usually lays six to eight, sometimes more, eggs, which both partners take turns incubating for nineteen to twenty-two days. The young, coloured black with a reddish head, are fed by the parents in the nest for two to three days, after which they swim about with the adult birds, keeping to the concealment of the thickets. The parents bring them insects and their larvae, spiders, small molluscs, etc., also the tender leaves of duckweed. In the autumn adult birds also eat small seeds. Sometimes the young of the second brood are supplied with food by those of the first brood.

Length: 33 cm. The male and female have like plumage. *Voice:* 'Kr-r-rk' or a note that sounds like 'kittick'. *Size of Egg:* 36.2—54.0 ×26.0—34.2 mm.

Coot

Rallidae

Fulica atra

The coot is the commonest member of the rail tribe and is found throughout all of Europe except the northernmost parts. Birds inhabiting eastern and northern Europe leave their nesting grounds in October/November and fly southwest, those of other parts of the Continent are resident or dispersive. In winter the coot is found on rivers or lakes that do not freeze over, often in huge flocks. They arrive at their breeding grounds in March and soon after the males wage fierce combat amongst themselves to win a mate. The paired birds then establish their territory and begin building a nest in reeds, rushes and grass, etc. It is located above the water, often floating on the surface, and leading to it from the water is a ramp of long leaves of rushes, reeds, etc. The structure is made of bits of stems and leaves and is sometimes covered with a roof of broken plant stems. The female usually lays six to nine eggs, which she and her partner take turns incubating for about twenty-two, sometimes as many as twenty-four, days. The young hatch successively, the first being led out on the water by the male, who after a few hours swims back to the nest for the next. The young are cared for and watched over by both parents. Their plumage is black but the head is orange-red with yellow-tipped feathers. The adult birds put the food they bring into their offspring's beaks. The diet consists mostly of green plant parts, in the autumn of seeds, and during the nesting period also of insects and their larvae, molluscs, crustaceans, spiders and other small invertebrates.

Length: 38 cm. The male and female have like plumage.
Voice: A clear 'tewk' or 'kt-kowk', also a short sharp 'skik'.
Size of Egg: 40.0—61.0 ×31.2—40.6 mm.

Lapwing

Charadriidae

Vanellus vanellus

The lapwing, one of the commonest of shore-birds is widespread throughout most of Europe, the only places where it does not nest being Portugal and Italy. In August/October it migrates to southwest Europe and northwest Africa but south and west European populations are resident. The lapwing returns to its nesting grounds in March, though it has often arrived by the end of February, its favourite sites being damp meadows and fields near water. In spring the lapwings perform their characteristic court-ship flights. The courtship display often takes place on the ground, the partners running around each other and the male often picking up a plant stalk with his bill and casting it behind him or to the side. In late March or April, sometimes also in May, the birds build a nest in a shallow depression in the ground in a meadow, field, on a raised spot in a swamp, etc. The structure is lined sparsely with leaves, plant stalks or small twigs. Like all shorebirds, the female usually lays four eggs, which she and her partner take turns incubating for twenty-four to twenty-eight days. The speckled nestlings remain in the nest for a day or two and then scatter in the neighbourhood, concealing themselves in clumps of grass when danger threatens. They begin flying at the age of five weeks, forming large flocks and roaming the countryside until they leave for their winter quarters. The diet consists of insects and their larvae, spiders, molluscs and the like as well as small bits of green vegetable matter and various seeds.

Length: 32 cm. The male and female have like plumage.
Voice: A ringing 'peese-weet', during the courtship display a note that sounds like 'pee-r-weet'.
Size of Egg: 37.8—60.4 ×27.8—36.1 mm.

118

Little Ringed Plover

Charadrius dubius

Charadriidae

The small, delightful little ringed plover inhabits all of Europe except the northernmost parts, being partial to sandy river banks and dry muddy situations near lakes and ponds. It is also fond of the edges of dried-out ponds with sandy bottoms, though there its nest is often flooded out by the rising water when the pond is filling. Sometimes it also makes its home in old sand pits where larger pools or a reservoir of water have formed at the bottom. August and September are the months when it leaves its breeding grounds for its winter quarters in Africa, south as far as the equator, returning again between the middle of April and beginning of May, as a rule. The nest, which the plover scrapes out by circling with its body, is a shallow depression in the ground, usually in gravel, amongst pebbles, etc. In muddy situations the depression is lined with small pebbles, small shells or pieces of twigs, plant stalks, etc. In open places the nest is hollowed out near a large stone or other conspicuous object that makes it easier to find. The four eggs, laid in April/May and a second time in June/July, are incubated by both partners for twenty-two to twenty-six days, the one relieving the other at short intervals. The young leave the nest as soon as they are dry and follow in the wake of their parents. At the age of twenty-one days they are already capable of flight. The diet of the little ringed plover consists of insects and their larvae, worms, spiders, molluscs, small crustaceans, etc. The bird seeks its prey on muddy ground, where it can often be seen running about rapidly.

Length: 15 cm. The male and female have like plumage.
Voice: A whistling 'tee-u', when excited or upset 'tree-a'.
Size of Egg: 25.5—35.5 ×20.9—24.9 mm.

Snipe

Scolopacidae

Gallinago gallinago

The small snipe inhabits all of western, central, eastern and northern Europe, but does not nest in the south. It leaves its breeding grounds in July—September, flying all the way to Africa, as far south as Uganda, though it also winters in large numbers in southwest, south and western Europe where it is sometimes resident. In March/April it returns again to its nesting grounds in marshy and damp meadows beside ponds and lakes. The nest is built in a clump of grass, in a hollow, in April or May, sometimes also June. The structure consists of dry stalks and long leaves and is concealed from above by drooping grass stems so that it is very hard to find. The clutch consists of four prettily coloured eggs, which the female incubates alone for nineteen to twenty-one days. While she sits on the nest the male often flies high up in the air, executing circles and spirals, and swooping down to the ground every now and then. When he plummets earthward he makes a characteristic drumming sound caused by the vibration of the outermost tail feathers. As soon as they are dry, the newly hatched nestlings scatter throughout the neighbourhood, concealing themselves in the tall vegetation. They are brownish-black with white spots, which is an excellent protective coloration. Both parents care for the young. At the age of twenty days the young begin to fly and in the autumn they join other snipes to form flocks. The diet consists mainly of insects and their larvae, also small molluscs, worms, spiders and other invertebrates. The snipe is a game bird.

Length: 26.5 cm. The male and female have like plumage.
Voice: The call it makes when on the ground sounds like 'chic-ka'.
Size of Egg: 35.0—42.9 ×26.3—31.0 mm.

Black-tailed Godwit

Scolopacidae

Limosa limosa

This robust shorebird is widespread in eastern Europe and is also found in the northern parts of Germany, Denmark, Holland, Belgium, the southern tip of Sweden, and in recent years in ever growing numbers also in central Europe. It also inhabits Iceland, the southeastern part of England and western part of France. In late July and August it leaves its nesting grounds for its winter quarters, mostly in the Mediterranean region but also on the western coast of Europe. March or April is the period when the black-tailed godwit returns to its breeding grounds, where it inhabits peat bogs, meadows near ponds and lakes as well as fields near water. After their arrival in small flocks, pairs of birds stake out their nesting territory. The courtship flight takes place in spring with the male flying in arcs above the nesting site, slowing every now and then, expanding his tail feathers and emitting a loud call. In April or May the birds build a simple nest in a shallow depression in grass. The female lays four speckled eggs which have excellent protective coloration that blends with their surroundings. She and her mate take turns incubating for twenty-four days. When relieving each other the birds alight on the ground several yards from the nest and make their way to it on foot, stopping frequently to look about them. Shortly after they have hatched the young scatter in the immediate vicinity, concealing themselves in the grass. The black-tailed godwit feeds on insects and their larvae, worms, molluscs, spiders and small crustaceans.

Length: 40.5 cm. The male and female have like plumage.
Voice: A note that sounds like 'reeka-reeka-reeka', repeated several times in succession.
Size of Egg: 45.3—63.9 ×32.4—41.3 mm.

Redshank

Scolopacidae

Tringa totanus

The redshank inhabits practically the whole of Europe, though it is absent in some parts of western and southern Europe, where it has a disrupted range. Its distribution is continuous in central, northern and eastern Europe — as far as the Amur River, and also in the British Isles. It winters chiefly in the Mediterranean and on Europe's west coast, leaving for these parts in July — September. Most of the British population is resident. Mid-March to April is the time of its return to the nesting grounds, where it is to be found mainly on wet meadows (also drier meadows with short grass located near lakes), marshes, swamps, and on the shores of stretches of water. The nest, a shallow depression in the ground, sparsely lined with dry plant stems and leaves from the vicinity, is carefully concealed in a clump of grass, etc. The nest is prepared by the male and lined by the female. In April or May, sometimes in June, the female lays four eggs, which she and her partner take turns incubating for twenty-two to twenty-five days. The young remain in the nest only one day, after which they scatter throughout the neighbourhood. They are watched over and cared for by both parents but gather their food themselves. They begin to fly when they are twenty-five days old and are fully mature by the time they are forty days old, after which they roam the countryside, forming groups on the muddy shores of ponds and lakes. The redshank's diet consists of insects and their larvae, spiders, worms, small molluscs and other invertebrates.

Length: 28 cm. The male and female have like plumage.
Voice: A flute-like 'tleu-hu-hu', when danger threatens a note that sounds like 'teuk' repeated several times in succession.
Size of Egg: 38.6 — 50.6 × 25.7 — 33.5 mm.

Common Sandpiper

Tringa hypoleucos

Scolopacidae

The small and agile sandpiper inhabits all of Europe excepting Iceland. In July—September it leaves for its winter quarters in the Mediterranean, sometimes also in western Europe, but mainly in Africa as far as Madagascar, returning again in mid-April to May. It is found in swampy situations and bogs, as well as on the shores of lakes, ponds and rivers. As a rule the birds arrive at their nesting grounds already in pairs. In spring the male flies close above the water, uttering loud cries. The nest is a shallow depression in the ground, usually under overhanging plants on the shore, under a bush and the like, near water, sometimes even on larger floating rafts of vegetation, close to a colony of gulls. The depression is lined with plant stalks and leaves. In May, sometimes also in June or July if the first clutch has been accidentally destroyed, the female lays four eggs which are incubated mostly by the male, the female relieving him on occasion. The young hatch after twenty-one to twenty-three days and leave the nest as soon as they are dry. The task of caring for the young also devolves upon the male, who leads them to food and provides them with protection while the female attends upon the family for only a few days. When they are a month old the young begin to fly, after which they join to form small groups that may be seen in marshy locations near water or in shallows, where they gather food. The diet consists of various worms, crustaceans, as well as insects and their larvae, spiders, centipedes and other small invertebrates.

Length: 19.5 cm. The male and female have like plumage.
Voice: When flying up in the air 'twee-see-see', during the courtship display a trilling 'titti-weeti, titti-weeti'.
Size of Egg: 32.2—40.2 × 22.5—28.0 mm.

Green Sandpiper

Tringa ochropus

Scolopacidae

The green sandpiper is a common wader of the southern and central parts of Scandinavia and northeast and eastern Europe. In late July or in August it leaves its breeding territory for its winter quarters, some birds stopping in western Europe and also in the Mediterranean but most flying on to Africa as far as the equator, occasionally even farther south. During the autumn migration flocks of these birds may be seen in plenty in central and western Europe. In its winter quarters the green sandpiper is found on the banks of large rivers and lakes and also by the seashore. The return to the nesting grounds is between the end of March and the beginning of May, the latest arrivals being those that nest in the northernmost regions. Soon after having arrived, the birds prepare for nesting. During the nesting period the green sandpiper occurs in marshland or on lakes and rivers with wooded banks, for unlike its relatives it nests in trees. However, it does not build the structure itself but takes over the abandoned nests of other birds. Like in other waders, the female lays four eggs which she and her partner take turns incubating for twenty to twenty-three days, hers being the more frequent stint. After they have hatched the young remain in the nest for one or two days and then tumble over the edge to the ground, usually falling unharmed on soft grass or moss. They are led to food and watched over by the parents until they attain maturity, after which the birds fly to marshland, ponds or lakes in open country. The diet consists mostly of small invertebrates.

Length: 23 cm. The male and female have like plumage. The white spots are absent in the winter garb.
Voice: A flute-like 'weet-tluitt'.
Size of Egg: 34.6—43.1 ×25.5—30.5 mm.

Black-headed Gull

Larus ridibundus

The black-headed gull is one of the commonest of European birds. It nests in central, western and eastern Europe, in Scandinavia and on the shores of Iceland. Northern and eastern populations fly south in July/August whereas gulls from the other parts of Europe may stay the winter or migrate to the Mediterranean. During the winter months the gulls seek out lakes and rivers that do not freeze over and often occur in large groups even in big cities, where people often feed them. They return to their breeding grounds in flocks, but already paired, during the months of March and April, nesting on lakes, ponds as well as the seashore. Black-headed gulls breed in large colonies comprising as many as a thousand birds. The nest is built by both partners on dry ground on islets or as a floating structure on water. The female usually lays three eggs which show marked variation in colour. These are incubated by both partners for twenty to twenty-three days. The speckled offspring remain in the nest a number of days, abandoning it sooner when disturbed, either concealing themselves in the surrounding vegetation or making their escape by swimming. Food is brought to the young by the male, who sometimes passes it first to the female to distribute. The young begin to fly at the age of five to six weeks, after which they roam the countryside in flocks. The diet consists of insects, worms, molluscs and other invertebrates as well as small vertebrates, also fish, frogs, etc. Sometimes the gulls also eat green plant parts and are fond of visiting cherry orchards.

Length: 37 cm. The male and female have like plumage. The head is coloured white in winter. *Voice:* A repeated 'kwarr' or short 'kroup', etc. *Size of Egg:* 43.0—66.0 ×31.3—42.1 mm.

Black Tern

Chlidonias niger

Laridae

Resembling a large swallow, the black tern may be seen flying gracefully above the water's surface. This tern inhabits eastern, central, southwestern and western Europe and occasionally nests in the British Isles. Sometimes, though rarely, it occurs also in the south of Sweden. Definitely a migrant, the black tern leaves for its winter quarters in August or the beginning of September, generally following a southwesterly course. Populations from the western parts of the Continent fly along the western coast of Europe and the shores of Spain to tropical Africa, eastern populations travel to Africa via the Nile. They return to their breeding grounds quite late — not till the end of April or beginning of May — seeking out ponds and lakes with dense vegetation, also peat bogs with small pools or swamps in lowland country. The black tern is a gregarious bird and nests in small colonies numbering several pairs. The nest of dry reeds is usually built on bent, flattened reeds in shallows as well as on small floating islets of vegetation. Often their nests on ponds are flooded by rising water or destroyed by large waves. Both partners share the task of construction. The female lays three, but sometimes only two eggs in May or June (if the nest is destroyed as late as July). Both partners take turns incubating for fourteen to seventeen days and both share the duties of feeding the young insects and their larvae as well as small fish, which they bring at frequent intervals. Flying insects are caught above the water's surface.

Length: 25 cm. The male and female have like plumage. *Voice:* A short 'kreek' or 'kitt'. *Size of Egg:* 30.5—40.2 ×22.5—27.4 mm.

Common Tern

Sterna hirundo

Laridae

The common tern inhabits practically all of Europe excepting the northernmost parts. It is absent, however, in some areas; for example it does not nest in central Spain. At the end of July, in more southerly parts of Europe also as late as September or October, it leaves for its winter quarters in the Persian Gulf, on the shores of the Red Sea and on the western coast of Africa, sometimes flying as far as Madagascar. It is an expert and skilled flier. The end of April or beginning of May marks its return to its breeding grounds, usually on large inland lakes or ponds as well as larger rivers, islands and the seacoast. A gregarious bird, it is usually seen in flocks and is also a colonial nester. The birds arrive at the nesting grounds in large groups and only then do they form pairs which perform courtship flights. The structure of the nest is made of small twigs, blades of grass, reeds and other plant parts, both green and dry, in a shallow depression. The nesting site is often a muddy location on an island or the mud deposit washed up by a river. In May or June the female lays three eggs, which are incubated by both partners twenty to twenty-four, sometimes even twenty-six days. The young are fed insects, insect larvae, other invertebrates and small fish by both parents. When searching for food the tern often hovers in one spot with head down, scanning the water's surface. As soon as it sights its prey it plunges into the water, often disappearing from sight, and then reappearing again with the victim in its beak. Young terns begin flying at the age of one month.

Length: 35 cm. The male and female have like plumage. *Voice:* Usually 'kree-err', also a short 'kirri-kirri'. *Size of Egg:* 35.3—48.0 ×25.0—32.8 mm.

Short-eared Owl

Asio flammeus

Strigidae

Open, damp meadows near ponds and lakes or marshes and moorland is where the short-eared owl makes its home. This attractive owl with short 'ears' of longish feathers inhabits all of northern, western, central and eastern Europe. In England it nests only in the northern half of the country and in Ireland it occurs only out of the breeding season. Birds of the northernmost regions are migrants, those that nest in more southerly parts are dispersive. In the autumn this owl may often be seen on fields. March to mid-April is the period of the short-eared owl's return to its breeding grounds. The nest is made of coarse plant stalks and the like in a shallow depression in the ground and lined with bits of leaves and finer plant parts. The structure is generally located in peaty or damp meadows. The eggs, four to seven, but as many as fourteen in years when rodents (food for the owl) are plentiful, are normally laid at forty-eight hour intervals. The female incubates alone for twenty-four to twenty-seven days, sitting on the eggs as soon as the first is laid; the young thus hatch successively one after the other. During this period the male stands guard close by and when the young have hatched he brings food for the whole family. The young leave the nest at the age of three to four weeks and take to the air when they are about five weeks old. When hunting prey the short-eared owl sometimes hovers motionless in the air in a single spot. Its victims are usually fieldmice and voles though it sometimes also captures small birds or amphibians and reptiles.

Length: 37 cm.
Wingspan: 103 to 107 cm. The male and female have like plumage.
Voice: A deep 'boo-boo' or 'kee-aw'.
Size of Egg: 35.1—45.0 ×29.0—33.0 mm. The eggs are white.

Kingfisher

Alcedo atthis

Alcedinidae

The kingfisher, one of the most attractively coloured of all birds, is found in all of Europe excepting the northernmost parts. In Scandinavia it occurs only in the south. It does not leave its breeding grounds for the winter but roams the countryside during the cold months, seeking water that does not freeze over, i.e. generally flowing rivers and streams. During the breeding season the kingfisher occurs on stagnant as well as flowing water of all kinds as long as these are bordered by a steep bank or embankment in which it digs its nesting burrow, which is usually forty to one hundred centimetres long. Both partners share the task of digging the burrow, which takes several days, using their beaks as digging implements and their feet to scrape the loosened matter out. The nesting chamber is not lined, but within a short time it becomes filled with the indigestible fragments of bones, fish scales, beetles' elytra, etc. which the birds cast up. The pairs have one brood in April — June and a second in June — July. The clutch consists of six to seven eggs and the female begins incubating as soon as the first is laid. The young hatch after eighteen to twenty-one days. During this period the male keeps his partner supplied with food and sometimes also relieves her. Both share the duties of feeding the young in the nesting chamber for twenty-three to twenty-seven days, continuing to bring them food a few days longer when they have fledged. The kingfisher catches small fish and also crustaceans and water insects. When hunting prey it dives into the water.

Length: 16.5 cm. The male and female have like plumage.
Voice: In flight a lengthy 'chee-kee' or short 'chee'.
Size of Egg: 20.3—24.8 ×16.7—20.0 mm. The eggs are pure white.

140

Bee-eater

Merops apiaster

The bee-eater, one of the most brightly coloured of European birds, is partial to warm areas and inhabits southern, southwestern and southeastern Europe. It also occurs in warmer parts of central and eastern Europe and very occasionally is dispersive in England and Scandinavia. All the European breeding grounds are abandoned in late August and September, when it leaves for its winter quarters in Africa or Arabia, returning again in April/May. It is to be found in open country in the vicinity of rivers, ponds or lakes, where it seeks as nesting habitat vertical mud or sand walls and banks, as well as abandoned sand quarries and sometimes quite small sand embankments. The bee-eater is a gregarious bird and colonial nester. Each pair of birds digs a burrow some 1.2—2 metres long, the task taking fourteen to twenty-one days. In May—July the female lays five to six, on occasion as many as ten eggs directly on the bare earth. Later, however, these rest on the indigestible particles the birds cast up. The male and female take turns incubating for twenty to twenty-two days and both feed the young for twenty to thirty days in the nest and a short while longer after they have fledged. The diet consists mostly of hymenopterous insects such as wasps, bumblebees and bees, also flying beetles, dragon-flies, cicadas, etc.; their chitinous armour is cast up by the birds. The bee-eater is an excellent and dexterous flier, light and graceful in flight but awkward and clumsy on land. Bee-keepers are not fond of the bee-eater for it can cause much damage to their bee colonies.

Length: 28 cm.
The male and female have like plumage.
Voice: In flight 'prruip'.
Size of Egg:
22.5—29.5
×17.6—23.6 mm.
The eggs are pure white.

Hoopoe

Upupidae

Upupa epops

The hoopoe inhabits practically all of Europe excepting northeastern Scandinavia and the British Isles; it also does not nest in Denmark and Iceland. However, it is dispersive in England and Finland. European populations leave in September for their winter quarters in tropical Africa, returning to their breeding grounds again in April. The hoopoe is found in open country with extensive meadows, especially near water, in the neighbourhood of ponds and lakes, and also in light deciduous woods. The nest is made in the hollows of trees, sometimes as much as six metres above, but sometimes also close to the ground, in a pile of rocks, in the rock dams of ponds, and the like. In May/June, sometimes also in July, the female lays six to seven eggs, which she alone incubates for sixteen to twenty days. Because the female starts incubating as soon as the first egg is laid the young hatch successively. Both parents feed their offspring in the nest for twenty-four to twenty-seven days, doling out the food in the following manner: one nestling awaits their arrival at the entrance hole and as soon as it receives its ration then the one behind it pushes its way to the opening, and so it continues, each returning to the end of the queue until its turn comes again. When the young have fledged the adult birds continue to feed them a short while longer. The hoopoe feeds mostly on insects and their larvae, which it digs out of the soil, as well as out of the droppings of cattle, with its long bill. However, it also gathers its prey on the surface, e.g. locusts, spiders, etc.

Length: 28 cm. The male and female have like plumage. *Voice:* The characteristic note 'poo-poo-poo'. *Size of Egg:* 23.1—30.3 ×16.3—19.8 mm.

Sand Martin or Bank Swallow

Riparia riparia

Hirundinidae

The slender sand martin inhabits all of Europe, Iceland being the only place where it does not nest. A migratory species, it leaves its European breeding grounds in August/September for its winter quarters in East Africa, returning again in late April or early May. It is found in open country with still stretches of water or flowing water courses with vertical mud or sand banks, shores, or abandoned sand quarries nearby, for it is in these that the sand martin, which lives in large colonies, digs its nest. The task is very hard and tiring for such a small and weak bird. It starts by perching on a small ledge and digging a hole with its beak. Later it also uses its feet to remove the mud or sand, working tirelessly until it has excavated a tunnel about one metre long terminated by a nesting hollow about ten centimetres in diameter. It is then lined with bits of straw and feathers, some of which are amazingly long, for example the wing quills of a hen. The female lays five to six eggs in May/June, occasionally a second time again in July, which she and her partner take turns incubating for twelve to fourteen days (sometimes, though rarely, as long as sixteen days). The young are supplied with food which the parents catch on the wing, for sixteen to twenty-three days in the nest. When the young have fledged the parents continue to feed them for two more weeks. The diet consists of various insects, which the birds catch on the wing above the water's surface. When feeding the young, however, they also seek their prey in sand quarries and near the nest.

Length: 12 cm. The male and female have like plumage.
Voice: In flight a note that sounds like 'tcherip'.
Size of Egg: 15.2—22.0 ×11.4—13.5 mm. The eggs are pure white.

Penduline Tit

Remiz pendulinus

Remizidae

The small penduline tit is widely distributed throughout eastern and southeastern Europe and the eastern part of central Europe; it also occurs in Italy, southern France and southern Spain. It is found near stagnant as well as flowing water edged thickly with shrubs and trees, whose dense crowns are the bird's favourite haunts; it is also partial to thickets and reeds. This tit is one of the best builders in the bird realm. In April/May the male starts building the nest, having previously found a suitable area and there selects a nice, thin but firm branch of some tree as a willow, aspen, or the like. First he brings one blade of grass and winds it round the branch, then he brings more and interlaces them to form the pear-shaped framework of the bag that will be the nest. His work attracts a mate who then assists him in the task. If he is not successful in attracting a partner he moves elsewhere. Together the pair of birds continue improving the nest, adding to the grass stems the fluffy seeds of poplars, willows, and the like, and joining the whole together with their saliva. The clutch of five to eight eggs is incubated by the female alone for twelve to fifteen days. During this time the male starts building another nest and tries to attract a further mate. The young are cared for only by the female, who feeds them for ten to fifteen days in the nest and a further ten days after they have fledged. The diet consists of various caterpillars, also spiders, mosquitoes, beetles, etc. In the autumn and winter months the penduline tit also feeds on small seeds and other vegetable matter.

Length: 11 cm. The male and female have like plumage. *Voice:* A long 'seeou' note, the song drawn-out, chattering. *Size of Egg:* 14.0—18.0 ×9.7—11.3 mm. The eggs are pure white.

Bearded Tit

Panurus biarmicus

Timaliidae

Thick reed-beds are the favourite haunts of the lovely bearded tit, widespread in south-eastern Europe as well as in eastern Spain and occurring isolatedly also in several places in central Europe. It also nests in France, Holland, Belgium and the east of England. It usually stays the winter in its breeding grounds but some individuals from the northerly regions fly southward at this time. It spends the entire life in the reed-beds bordering lakes and large ponds, and in swamps. The nest, a fairly large structure, is built in April or May and a second time in June/July amidst thick reed-beds, in a clump of grass or rushes, often just above the water's surface. Both partners share the task of construction, bringing in their bills bits of reed stems, the long leaves of reeds and rushes and other marsh plants and weaving them firmly together. The nesting hollow is lined with bird feathers. The female generally lays five to seven eggs, which both partners take turns incubating for twelve to thirteen days, though sometimes the young hatch even after ten days. They are fed insects, which the parents catch amongst the reeds, for ten to thirteen days in the nest and a further fourteen days or so after they have fledged. The family remains together for about three weeks, after which the young fly off and the adult birds start building a new nest preparatory to raising a second brood. The diet consists of small invertebrates. In the autumn and winter months the bearded tit feeds mostly on the seeds of water and marsh plants.

Length: 16.5 cm. The female has a grey-brown head and does not have the black patch on the cheek,
Voice: Courting note 'cheen', alarm note 'tching', song soft chattering note.
Size of Egg: 14.5—19.2 × 13.0—15.0 mm.

Dipper

Cinclus cinclus

All of Europe, excepting the eastern part, is the home of the dipper. Even though it is widely distributed throughout the whole of Scandinavia it does not nest in the northern parts of central Europe. It usually stays the winter in its breeding grounds. The dipper is found beside rapid-flowing streams, and in the mountains even above the tree line. In April/May it looks about for a suitable nesting territory, often establishing itself there for years, and starts building a nest — in a wall beside a brook, in cracks under a footbridge, in a hole between rocks, sometimes even behind a waterfall. The size of the nest depends on the size of the cavity, for the dipper fills the entire space with moss and bits of water plants. It is interesting to note that the bird dives underwater for the plants and that it dips the moss in water too. Both partners share the task of building the nest, which is a domed structure with the entrance at the side. The female lays four to six eggs and in all probability incubates them alone for fourteen to seventeen days. Whether she is aided in this task by the male or not has not yet been sufficiently proved. However, both birds attend upon the young for eighteen to twenty-four days in the nest and a short while longer after they have fledged. When foraging for food, the dipper scampers into the water and gathers insect larvae and small crustaceans on the bottom, even catching small fish now and then. It runs about expertly with the aid of its wings and when the current is too strong it catches hold of larger stones with its claws.

Length: 18 cm. The male and female have like plumage.
Voice: A short 'zit', song similar to that of the wren, consisting of piping and chattering notes.
Size of Egg: 23.8—27.7 ×17.4—20.1 mm.

Bluethroat

Muscicapidae

Luscinia svecica

The bluethroat is widespread mostly in eastern and northern Europe, also nesting rarely in central and western Europe but not in England. It is also found in several places in central Spain. There are two subspecies that differ from each other in coloration. One is *Luscinia svecica svecica*, which inhabits Scandinavia, Finland and the USSR up to about 60° latitude North and has a russet patch in the centre of the blue throat-patch, and the other is *Luscinia svecica cyanecula*, which inhabits the other parts of Europe and has a white spot in the centre of its blue throat-patch. During the autumn and spring migration flights the former appears in large numbers in central Europe on its trip to North Africa, which is the winter quarters of the second subspecies as well. The birds leave their breeding grounds in late August or September and return again between the middle of March and mid-April. Their favourite nesting grounds are swampy areas thickly covered with bushes and reeds. The nest is built in May/June on the ground or close above it, well concealed in undergrowth or thickets. It is made of plant stems and fine roots and is erected by the female, according to existing observations. Whether she is aided by the male or not is not definitely known. The clutch consists of five to six eggs, which the female generally incubates alone for twelve to fourteen days. The young are fed in the nest by both parents for thirteen to fourteen days and a further two weeks after they have fledged. The diet of both young and adult birds consists of small invertebrates.

Length: 14 cm. The female has a dull throat patch compared with the male.
Voice: Courting call 'tac', song a warbling 'wheet'.
Size of Egg: 16.4—20.7 × 12.5—15.1 mm.

154

♂

River Warbler

Muscicapidae

Locustella fluviatilis

The inconspicuous, slender river warbler inhabits eastern Europe and the eastern parts of central Europe, its distribution extending eastward as far as the Urals. It also occurs rarely along the southern edge of Sweden and the Danube marks the southern boundary of its distribution. Definitely a migratory species, it sets out for its winter quarters in August or September, generally travelling southward along the Nile and wintering in tropical East Africa, though it sometimes flies as far as the eastern coast of South Africa. In its winter quarters it seeks out places with dense vegetation alongside lakes and rivers. In the middle of May it reappears again in its breeding grounds next to rivers bordered with dense thickets, popular haunts being thick stands of willow, alder and other trees with lush tall vegetation, also woodlands bordering rivers. This is where the bird builds its nest, usually close above the ground. It is made of dry stems and leaves and lined with fine plant parts, moss and animal hairs. Both partners share in the work. In May or June, occasionally even in July, the female lays four to five eggs, which she incubates for thirteen days mostly by herself, though the male probably relieves her now and then. The young are fed insects, insect larvae and other invertebrates by both parents for about two weeks in the nest and a further two weeks after fledging. The diet of the adult birds also consists solely of animal food. The river warbler is usually less often seen than heard. When singing the male perches on the highest branch of a bush.

Length: 12.5 cm. The male and female have like plumage.
Voice: Song that sounds like 'zwee'.
Size of Egg: 18.0—22.3 ×14.0—16.8 mm.

Savi's Warbler

Locustella luscinioides

Muscicapidae

The slender Savi's warbler inhabits western, southwestern, and all of central and eastern Europe and is also distributed in Italy and Sicily but does not nest in the British Isles. It is dispersive in Sweden. Even though it is found in most parts of Europe there are many regions where it is not to be seen. A migrant, it sets out in the autumn, generally in September, for its winter quarters in Africa in the Nile region and in East Africa; eastern populations fly also to southwest Asia. The birds return to their breeding grounds in the second half of April, seeking out large and thick reed beds on lakes and larger ponds, also reeds in inaccessible bogs, marshes, swamps and river deltas. The male's song is generally heard in the evening, sometimes, however, also in the daylight hours. When singing he perches on the tip of a reed stem, but always in thick vegetation so that it is difficult to spot him. In May or June the male builds the nest unaided in thick reeds or grass twenty to thirty centimetres above the water's surface. It is made of reed and timothy-grass stems, which, however, are not woven round the surrounding reeds, and measures about fifteen centimetres across at the top, narrowing towards the bottom. The female lays three to six eggs and incubates them alone for twelve to fourteen days. Both parents feed the young insects, insect larvae and other invertebrates for twelve to fourteen days on the nest and about ten days longer after they have fledged. The diet of the adult birds also consists of various invertebrates found in reeds, rushes, etc.

Length: 14 cm. The male and female have like plumage.
Voice: A note that sounds like 'tswik', song a chattering 'arrr'.
Size of Egg: 17.5—21.5 × 13.6—15.4 mm.

Grasshopper Warbler

Muscicapidae

Locustella naevia

The inconspicuous grasshopper warbler is distributed throughout most of Europe from northern Spain to southern Sweden and Finland. It does not nest in Italy or the Balkan Peninsula, but inhabits the British Isles. Its favourite haunts are tall, dense shrubbery, stands of willow and alder with thick grass cover, marshy meadows and thickets bordering lakes, ponds and dead-end branches of rivers. Here it lives its retiring mode of life, being seen only on rare occasions. More often one can hear the song of the male, who perches on a raised stem as he sings, his buzzing note sometimes continuing without interruption a full three minutes. The grasshopper warbler is a migrant and leaves for its winter quarters in North Africa or southwestern Asia in August or September, returning to its breeding grounds again in late April or beginning of May. The courting period begins shortly after its arrival, with the male running about on the ground in front of the female, ruffling his feathers and spreading his wings and tail. The nest, well concealed under a grass tussock or a thick shrub, is built in May or June by both partners. It is made of grass blades or reeds and is fairly deep. The clutch consists of four to five eggs, which are incubated twelve to fourteen days mostly by the female, though the male relieves her now and then. The young are cared for by both parents, who bring them various small invertebrates. The adults' diet is the same. The young leave the nest after nine days but continue to be fed by the parents a further two weeks.

Length: 12.5 cm. The male and female have like plumage.
Voice: Courting call a note that sounds like 'twhit', song resembling 'seerrrrrr . . .'.
Size of Egg: 16.0—20.3 ×12.5—14.8 mm.

Great Reed Warbler
Acrocephalus arundinaceus

Muscicapidae

The great reed warbler, largest of the European warblers, has a wide distribution embracing all of Europe excepting the British Isles and Scandinavia, though it occurs in rare instances in the southern tip of Sweden. It leaves its European breeding grounds in August/September for its winter quarters in equatorial and South Africa, returning again in spring at the beginning of May. Its favourite haunts are large reed-beds in ponds, pools, lakes and river deltas. Plentiful throughout its whole range, it is easily identified from afar by the male's typical song, or rather strident note, whose loudness few other birds can match. In May — July the female, unaided by the male, builds a fairly large nest of reed stems woven round two to six tall reeds which serve as supporting 'pillars'. She either pulls out of the water the old reed leaves of which the nest is made or else thoroughly soaks them so that they are pliable and thus more easily woven. The nest is generally located some fifty to one hundred centimetres above the water's surface. The clutch consists of four to five eggs, which both partners take turns incubating for fourteen to fifteen days; both also share the duties of caring for the young. These are fed twelve to fourteen days in the nest and a further two weeks after fledging. The diet consists solely of small invertebrates, mostly insects and insect larvae, spiders and small molluscs, which the great reed warbler gathers on water and swamp plants.

Length: 19 cm. The male and female have like plumage. *Voice:* Alarm note 'karrr karrr', song a loud and strident 'karra karra, krik, krik, gurk', etc. *Size of Egg:* 19.5—26.3 ×15.1—17.6 mm.

Reed Warbler

Acrocephalus scirpaceus

Muscicapidae

The reed warbler is among the commonest of all European warblers. It inhabits most of Europe but does not nest in Ireland or Holland; in Scandinavia it occurs only in the south and in Finland only in the south-western parts. A migrant species, it leaves its breeding grounds in late September or early October, wintering as far away as tropical Africa, mainly in the east. In the second half of April or beginning of May it returns to its nesting sites in reeds bordering ponds and lakes as well as in swampy locations. The nest is not often built above water, being sometimes located quite far away from it. It is placed between several strong reed stems, usually three or four, though sometimes it may also be built amidst the thin branches of a shrub, the walls of the nest being woven round these supports. Shaped like a deep basket, so that neither the eggs nor the young nestlings can fall out even if there is a strong wind, it is woven of finer material than that of the great reed warbler. The female lays four to five eggs in May or June (in rare instances even in July or August if the first nest is destroyed) and she and her partner take turns incubating for a period of eleven to twelve days, sometimes also fourteen days. Both likewise share the duties of feeding the young — eleven to fourteen days in the nest and a further two weeks after fledging. They also shield the young with their bodies against rain as well as the scorching heat of the sun. The food consists of insects and insect larvae, spiders, small gastropod molluscs, and the like. The reed warbler is not particularly shy.

Length: 12.5 cm. The male and female have like plumage.
Voice: Song not loud, something like 'chirruc-chirruc, jag-jag-jag', etc.
Size of Egg: 16.3—21.4 ×12.4—14.7 mm.

Sedge Warbler

Acrocephalus schoenobaenus

Muscicapidae

The sedge warbler inhabits all of Europe excepting the Iberian Peninsula and Iceland. A migrant species, it leaves its breeding grounds in September/October for its winter quarters in tropical Africa, flying south as far as the Transvaal, and returning again in the second half of April. It is found in abundance on the banks of lakes and ponds in reeds, tall grass and nettles as well as thickets. Even though it is well concealed in thick vegetation its presence is revealed soon after its arrival by its song, somewhat reminiscent of that of the reed warbler. However, whereas the latter perches on some elevated spot as it sings, the sedge warbler flies up into the air with widespread wings and tail and then dives downward again in a slanting line.

In May or June the paired birds build a fairly large nest in thickets, reeds, or tall grass near water, sometimes also directly above the water. The structure is made of plant stalks, roots and moss and lined with plant fluff, animal hairs, and the like. It is erected by both partners but the major share of the task falls to the female, who, when it is completed, lays four to five, sometimes as many as seven eggs, which she incubates alone for twelve to thirteen days. Both partners, however, care for their offspring, feeding them insects, insect larvae, spiders and small gastropod molluscs. The young leave the nest at the age of ten to thirteen days, remaining and hiding in the surrounding vegetation, where their parents continue to bring them food for another ten to fourteen days.

Length: 12.5 cm. The male and female have like plumage.
Voice: Song similar to that of the reed warbler but the sequences are more frequently repeated and sound like 'tuc tuc tuc'.
Size of Egg: 15.7—20.5 × 11.9—15.0 mm.

166

Meadow Pipit

Anthus pratensis

Motacillidae

The meadow pipit is widespread throughout all of western, central, northern and north-eastern Europe and is also found in Italy. It inhabits swampy meadows, locations near water covered with short grass, and also mountain meadows. Birds from more north-erly parts are migrant. Some birds spend the winter in western Europe, but most travel to the Mediterranean, leaving their breeding grounds in September — November. March or April is the time of the birds' return to their nesting territories, their arrival being shortly made known by the song of the male, who flies up in the air as he sings and as he finishes descends to the ground in a straight, vertical line. In May/June, occasionally as early as the end of April, the meadow pipit builds a nest on the ground, well concealed in a clump of grass, where it is practically invisible. The structure of the nest is made of grass stems, reeds, moss, lichens, and is almost always lined with ani-mal hairs. The clutch generally consists of four to five eggs, which the female incubates alone for twelve to fourteen days. The young are fed by both parents — mostly insects, insect larvae, small spiders, and the like. They leave the nest at the age of eleven to thirteen days. About fourteen days later the young are fully independent and the adult birds usually prepare to raise a second brood. The diet consists chiefly of hymenopterous insects and small beetles, as well as spiders and other small invertebrates. In the autumn and winter months the meadow pipit also feeds on various small seeds.

Length: 14.5 cm. The male and female have like plumage.
Voice: Song that sounds like 'tseep . . .', also a call resembling 'tissip'.
Size of Egg: 17.2—21.4 ×13.0—15.7 mm.

Yellow Wagtail

Motacilla flava

Motacillidae

All of Europe, excepting Ireland and Iceland, is home to the attractively coloured yellow wagtail. A migrant, it leaves in August/September for tropical Africa, flying as far as Capetown. In the autumn flocks numbering as many as a thousand birds may be seen beside ponds and lakes, where they pass the night in the reeds. On the return trip at the end of March or beginning of April they converge in smaller flocks, which soon break up into pairs that stake out their particular nesting territories, which the male aggressively defends against all other males. The yellow wagtail is partial to extensive damp and swampy meadows, the grass-covered banks of rivers, ponds and lakes, especially in lowland areas. However, it may also be found on the edges of fields near water. In May/June the female builds a nest on the ground, well concealed by a clump of grass which often forms a kind of roof. The structure is made of grass stems and lined with animal hairs, sometimes also with plant wool and occasionally small feathers. The male watches as the female goes about her task but does not help her in any way. The clutch usually consists of four to five eggs, which the female incubates alone for thirteen to fourteen days, the male meantime staying close by. The young are fed by both parents. They leave the nest at the age of seven to eleven days though still incapable of flight, and continue to be fed by the parents some two weeks more. The diet consists of locusts, small species of beetles, caterpillars, also spiders, small gastropod molluscs, etc.

Length: 16.5 cm. The female is not as brightly coloured as the male and her head is olive-green.
Voice: A ringing, one-syllable note 'tsweep'.
Size of Egg: 16.3—21.0 ×12.0—15.3 mm.

Corn Bunting

Emberiza calandra

Emberizidae

The corn bunting inhabits all of Europe except the northern and northeastern parts. In Scandinavia it is found only in the south-western part of Sweden. Throughout most of its range it is resident, during the winter months also dispersive. First to return to the nesting grounds — open meadows in the vicinity of rivers as well as fields dotted with bushes — is the male, who selects and establishes his nesting territory. This often takes place as early as the end of March, but the beginning of April is the more usual time. Here, he then perches on the tip of a tall plant or some other elevated spot and sings his song. The female arrives several days later and shortly after begins building a nest in a shallow depression on the ground underneath a clump of overhanging grass. The structure is made of roots and dry grass stems and is lined with small stems, animal hairs and also plant wool. In May or June the female lays four to five eggs, which she incubates alone for twelve to fourteen days. Upon hatching the young are fed only by the female for the first four days, after which time she is aided in her task by the male. Sometimes, however, the male has several mates. The young leave the nest at the age of nine to twelve days, though as yet incapable of flight, and conceal themselves in the vicinity in clumps of grass, being sought out there by the parents, who continue to bring them food. During the nesting season the corn bunting's diet consists mostly of small invertebrates, later the bird feeds chiefly on small grass seeds as well as grain kernels and green plant parts.

Length: 18 cm. The male and female have like plumage.
Voice: Courting note that sounds like 'chip', song rapid, dry jingle, resembling rattling bunch of keys.
Size of Egg: 19.0—28.6 ×16.0—19.5 mm.

Reed Bunting

Emberiza schoeniclus

Emberizidae

All of Europe, except Iceland, is the home of the reed bunting. In western, southern and southeastern Europe it is resident, whereas north and east European populations leave in October, as a rule passing the winter in the Mediterranean region. In central Europe some birds are resident and some are migrant, flying for the winter to Italy, France or Spain. The reed bunting is found in marshland and swampy locations, beside ponds and lakes where there are large reed-beds and also grassy areas. It may be seen again in its nesting grounds in March. In April/May the female, unaided by her mate, builds a nest in a dry spot in a clump of grass or in dry reeds, also on the dam of a pond or in a field near water. The well concealed structure is made of dry grass stems, reed leaflets and other plant material and lined with fine stems and animal hairs. The clutch usually consists of four to six eggs, which the female incubates twelve to fourteen days mostly by herself. Only on occasion is she relieved by the male. Both parents feed the young, bringing them mostly insects and insect larvae found on reed stems or grass. The young leave the nest at the age of eleven to thirteen days but continue to be fed by the parents a further two weeks or so. When their offspring are fully independent the adult birds have a second brood, generally in June/July, though occasionally as late as August. Besides the small invertebrates that comprise the diet during the nesting season, adult birds feed mostly on the seeds of various plants and on parts of green shoots.

Length: 15 cm. The female does not have the black head and white breast. In his non-breeding plumage the male resembles the female.
Voice: Courting note that sounds like 'tseek', song short and resembling 'tseek-tseek-tseek-tississisk'.
Size of Egg: 17.5—23.3 ×13.4—15.7 mm.

174

PROTECTION OF WATER BIRDS

Many water birds are becoming increasingly rare. Some species have become a target of extermination because they are considered harmful by man. Heading the list are those that are fish-eaters, for, according to fishermen, they pose a threat to their livelihood. Large European colonies of cormorants, herons and pelicans no longer exist thanks to man's intervention and only in a few places, e.g. in the Danube and Rhône deltas, are these birds still fairly plentiful, although even here they are being exterminated by fishermen and their numbers are constantly declining. Changes wrought by man in the natural swamp environment have caused water and marshland birds to move away. Smaller colonies of herons, chiefly the grey heron, are retaining a foothold thanks to protective measures in various parts of Europe. Cormorants, however, are very rare nesters in the interior. Water birds and members of the order Ciconiiformes are being driven out by the draining of swamps and marshes which provided them with shelter and where they found food. Thus the crane, which nowadays nests only rarely in the lake country of West Germany and Poland, was driven out of western and central Europe and is completely absent in western Europe. Also the rails and certain waders have disappeared from such drained lands in central and western Europe. The osprey is another species that has become rare, as have other raptorial birds nesting near bodies of water.

Birds are a part of nature's realm and man should not permit the decimation of further species of birds and other animals, for once extinct they cannot be replaced.

Effective protection and conservation of water birds, many of which are game birds, should be first and foremost the concern of the hunters themselves. There would soon be no ducks to hunt if they were not protected. They would soon be exterminated. Also species that are more rare or that nest only sporadically in a given region should not be hunted at all and hunters should be required to pass a test showing their knowledge of birds before being issued with a licence. During the breeding season it is essential that the greatest possible quiet be maintained on ponds, lakes, pools, and in their immediate vicinity so that birds are not disturbed unnecessarily while incubating and so that they can care for their offspring as they should. Great harm can be caused by freely roaming dogs, which flush sitting ducks or other birds, some of which abandon their nests altogether if disturbed more frequently. Roaming cats can likewise cause much damage. Also important, however, is to provide sufficient places of concealment. Ducks, and naturally other birds, too, need to feel safe and this is possible only in thick stands of reeds, rushes, and grass. That is why the continuous belt of the previous year's reeds should be preserved on the edges of all ponds, and on lakes where reeds and rushes are harvested they should be left standing in some spots where ducks and other water birds can seek shelter, especially in spring before the new vegetation has grown in. Most important for ducks are open stretches of water, only partly covered with reeds and low clumps of grass. To leave some of these untouched, therefore, is a must and need in no way be an obstacle to successful lake management. Old stands are a good shelter also for grebes, rails, gulls and many other species of birds. Reeds that are left standing, however, should be located alongside shallows where the offspring of various species of birds mainly forage for food. Another cardinal rule should be never to cut reeds during the nesting period for such spring harvesting is responsible for the death of many young nestlings or the destruction of eggs as yet unhatched.

A suitable spot for ducks to nest is an islet or several islets on a larger pond; these islets may also be at the edge of the pond. Overgrown islets have a great many advantages. Ducks, especially diving ones, are fond of building nests there close to water, and on such islets the nests are not in danger of being flooded if the water level rises. Furthermore, vermin find it difficult to reach such islets and in addition to that the birds are not as exposed to disturbance as on the shore. Also clumps of grass on the shore are a good place for ducks to build their nests, but these are sometimes flooded when the water level in the pond rises.

Flooding is not so frequent on lakes. For that reason wooden nest-boxes can be placed to good advantage in reeds and rushes bordering the lake as well as on islets, where many species of ducks will lay eggs and rear young ducklings. The nest-boxes should be located above the highest probable water line and a wooden ramp with cross-bars should be affixed to the opening. This makes it easy for the birds to enter no matter what the level of the water, which thus cannot destroy the eggs or affect the successful outcome of their hatching. The nest-boxes should be about seventy centimetres long, forty centimetres wide and forty centimetres high, with an entry hole twelve to fifteen centimetres in diameter. They should be impregnated with a water-resistant

Fig. 6. Nest-box for ducks.

substance so that they are impervious to damage from damp. The nesting hole itself, which should be separated by a low wooden partition, should be lined with some turf and soft, dry leaves and moss. For ducks that nest in tree cavities, e.g. goldeneyes, the nest-box should be placed in a tree beside water. Such a box should be about fifty to seventy centimetres high, thirty-five centimetres wide and the entry hole twelve centimetres across. These nest-boxes should be lined similarly and a shallow depression made so that the eggs do not roll out.

On ponds we can also provide ducks with flat feeding boxes that either float on the water or else are attached to wooden piles about thirty centimetres above the surface and reached by means of slanting ramps. A roof above the box serves to keep the food dry when it rains. Furthermore, when bogs and swamps are being drained some such spots should be left intact in certain areas so that water and marshland birds which nest there do not move away, thus impoverishing the local fauna and characteristic stamp of the given countryside. Every country in Europe should set aside and protect by law certain specific areas with lakes and ponds and their typical fauna and flora.

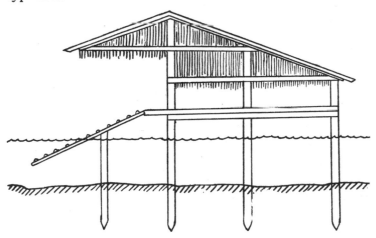

Fig. 7. Feeding box for ducks.

BIBLIOGRAPHY

Atkinson-Willes, G.L.: (ed.) *Wild Fowl in Great Britain*. Monographs of the Nature Conservancy no. 3., HM Stationery Office, London, 1963.

Austin, O.L.: *Birds of the World*. London, 1963.

Bannerman, D.A.: *The Birds of the British Isles*. Edinburgh, 1953—63.

Bayliss Smith, S.: *British Waders in their Haunts*. G. Bell & Sons Limited, London, 1950.

Benson, S.V.: *The Observer's Book of British Birds*. London, 1937.

Braun, B. and Singer, A.: *The Hamlyn Guide to Birds of Britain and Europe*. London, 1970.

Delacour, J.: *The Waterfowl of the World*; Vols 1—4. Country Life Limited, London.

Dementiev, G.P., et al: *Birds of the USSR*. In Russian. Moscow, 1951—54.

Grassé, O.: *Traité de Zoologie*, vol. XV. Oiseaux, Paris, 1950.

Harrison, J.: *A Wealth of Wild Fowl (A 'Survival Book')*. Andre Deutsch, London, 1967.

Heinroth, O. et M.: *Die Vögel Mitteleuropas*. Frankfurt a.M., 1966—68.

Hochbaum, H.A.: *Travels and Traditions of Waterfowl*. University of Minnesota Press, Minneapolis, 1955.

Jespersen, P.: *Migration of Birds*. London, 1950.

Johnsgard, P.A.:*Handbook of Waterfowl Behavior*. Cornell University Press, Ithaca, New York, 1965.

Lincoln, F.: *Migrating of Birds*. London, 1950.

Peterson, R.T., Mountfort, G., Hollom, P.A.: *Birds of Britain and Europe*. London, 1971.

Rudebeck, G.: *Studies of Bird Migration*. London, 1950.

Schütz, E.: *Vom Vogelzug*. Frankfurt am Main, 1952.

Scott, P.: *The Swans, Geese and Ducks of the British Isles*. Annual Report of the Wildfowl Trust. Slimbridge, 1950—51.

Scott, P. & Boyd, H.: *Wild Fowl of the British Isles*. Country Life Limited, London, 1957.

Thomson, A.: *A New Dictionary of Birds.* London and Edinburgh, 1964.

Van Ijzendoorn, A.L.: *The Breeding Birds of the Netherlands.* Leiden, 1950.

Voous, K.K.: *Atlas of European Birds.* London, 1960.

Witherby, H.F.: *The Handbook of British Birds.* London, 1938—41.

INDEX OF COMMON NAMES

INDEX OF LATIN NAMES